W9-CZE-708

THE UNIVERSE
AS JOURNEY

BD
111
.U55

THE UNIVERSE AS JOURNEY

CONVERSATIONS WITH W. NORRIS CLARKE, S.J.

Edited by
GERALD A. McCOOL, S.J.

FORDHAM UNIVERSITY PRESS
New York
1988

© Copyright 1988 by FORDHAM UNIVERSITY
All rights reserved
LC 88–80357
ISBN 0–8232–1208–4

Printed in the United States of America

CONTENTS

THE UNIVERSE
AS JOURNEY

INTRODUCTION

As one of Fordham's oldest and most prestigious lectures, the Suarez Lecture is customarily given by a distinguished philosopher from another university. In 1985, however, to celebrate Norris Clarke's thirty years of service in its philosophy department, Fordham broke with a long-established tradition and invited him to give the Suarez Lecture. Not only did Father Clarke consent to do so; he also agreed to make its theme a reflection on the philosophical significance of his own career as a student and teacher of metaphysics. The result was a rich and concise *summa* of his thought, which he entitled "Fifty Years of Metaphysical Reflection: The Universe as Journey."

In the course of the lecture the significance of its title became very clear. His own philosophy, Father Clarke told his audience, had its roots in an inborn passion for unity and an ear for the inner harmony of the universe. He owed to them his natural predisposition for metaphysics. For metaphysics, he continued, was a vision of the world as an intelligible totality; its task was to spell out systematically the philosopher's vision of reality as a meaningful whole. His own Thomistic metaphysics had been the outcome both of his natural predisposition and of his own intellectual history. He had been introduced to Thomism as a young Jesuit seminarian on the island of Jersey, and had deepened his knowledge of it as a graduate student at the University of Louvain. His own personal form of Thomism was built upon the primacy of the act of existence and St. Thomas' Neoplatonic participation metaphysics.

Under the inspiration of phenomenology and existentialism, he had made personal, or rather interpersonal, experience the starting-point of his philosophy. Action, through which a partner in dialogue made himself present to his interlocutor as a dynamic existent, could then become the criterion of a

1

being's reality. Furthermore, as the Transcendental Thomists had seen so clearly, the dynamic finality of the questioning mind, which manifested itself in personal experience, was unrestricted in its scope. It followed therefore that the dynamism of the philosopher's own inquiring mind justified his affirmation of Infinite Being as the ground and end of his ability to question.

Metaphysics, Father Clarke continued, begins with a guiding image whose implications had to be worked out and justified with scientific conceptual rigor. The guiding image that had directed his own reflection from the outset of his career was the image of the universe as a journey. In that cosmic journey all being went forth from the One and returned to the One. For a disciple of St. Thomas the One was God, the Infinite Being. Sharing His infinite reality with a community of finite agents through continuous creative action, God directed this community of finite agents back to Himself as the final cause of their own activity.

Norris Clarke's personal philosophical journey, both as a student nourished by the several streams of contemporary Thomism and as a teacher and writer engaged in dialogue with contemporary American philosophy, had provided him with the metaphysical structure required for the scientific articulation of his directing vision. This was an original and coherent Thomistic synthesis whose elements were six major metaphysical positions: the unrestricted dynamism of the mind; the primacy of the act of existence; the participation structure of reality; the role of action as the criterion of reality; the good as the final cause of action; and the person, considered both as the starting-point of philosophy and as the intelligible ground of the categories needed for a flexible contemporary metaphysics.

As a special tribute to Father Clarke, Fordham decided that, in 1985, the Suarez Lecture should be incorporated into a Suarez Institute. On the morning and the afternoon following the lecture itself, three distinguished philosophers read papers on topics germane to Father Clarke's own philosophical preoccupations. Each of the invited speakers, John D. Caputo of Villanova, Lewis S. Ford of Old Dominion, and John E. Smith of Yale, addressed his topic from a different point of view. Professor Caputo stands in the tradition of Heidegger; Professor Ford is associated with the stream of process metaphysics that traces its origin to Whitehead; and Professor Smith is a distinguished contributor to American philosophy of religion. Following the lectures, a lively discussion took place in which the lecturers, the audience, and Father Clarke himself participated.

Thus the three essays that follow the text of Father Clarke's lecture in this volume make up a highly enlightening set of "conversations with Norris Clarke" centered upon the two poles of his philosophy: the human person and God. The link between the personal subject and the Being beyond finite beings reached through the unrestricted drive of his human mind, the metaphysics of God's simplicity and immutability, and the ontological and cosmological journeys of the mind to God are critically re-examined in the three succeeding essays. Valuable as each essay is, the group taken in itself gains in interest and significance through the unity that comes to the collected essays from their place in an ongoing conversation with Father Clarke. Each of them, from its own point of view, presents a distinct challenge to Norris Clarke's metaphysics of the human person, being, action, finality and God—a challenge to which he responds in the final section of this book.

The first essay, John Caputo's "Being and the Mystery of the Person," is a profound and deeply moving phenomenological reflection on the human face. The human face, he tells us, is a sur-face, a surface over an abyss. When the meaning of the human face discloses itself, through phenomena like lying and suffering, we experience the constant self-revelation and self-concealment of Being. Both Being and person therefore confront us with a mystery. Unlike Father Clarke, however, for whom the mystery of Being, manifested through the person, points to the super-conceptual intelligibility of Infinite *Esse*, Professor Caputo finds the mystery of Being inseparably

THE UNIVERSE AS JOURNEY

bound up with ambiguity. Like Father Clarke, Professor Caputo believes that the philosopher finds in the person a privileged starting-point for his reflection. For the experience of the person, through whom Being "sounds," gives him access to the twofold mystery of person and Being.

Yet Professor Caputo's phenomenological hermeneutics of Being, carried out in the tradition of Heidegger, does not reach the same conclusion as a Thomistic reflection on the human person. The person revealed through a phenomenology of the human face does not turn out to be the intelligent subsisting existent which Father Clarke equates with the acting person. Nor is the Being, which constantly reveals and conceals itself as it "sounds" through the person, what St. Thomas meant by being, the act of *esse*. It is quite true that *Dasein*, thrown into a contingent, ambiguous world, becomes aware of its constant effort to transcend itself through its conscious, free intentionality. Yet that experience gives us no assurance that the goal of *Dasein*'s transcendence is God. Neither is there any warrant for Father Clarke's firm conviction that the human intelligence, which ceaselessly raises the question about the Being beyond beings, is an unrestricted drive to Infinite *Esse*.

On the contrary, the ambiguous Being, which reveals and conceals itself through the lying or suffering face, allows us no more than the right to give the world its ultimate interpretation through our own free decision. It does not support Father Clarke's contention that an authentic person-centered metaphysics gives evidence that the world is an intelligible whole. In short, Professor Caputo's phenomenology of the human face raises a disturbing question for contemporary Thomists. Even in the hands of its best representatives, has their metaphysics met the challenge of Heidegger's "hermeneutics of Being"? If it has not, how can they validate their claim that the Being which "sounds" through the human person is the *Esse* of St. Thomas?

In Professor Ford's "Process and Thomist Views Concerning Divine Perfection" the focus of the conversation shifts from the finite person to the metaphysics of God's reality. For Norris Clarke, action, through which being "expresses itself," is the criterion for a being's reality. Since "intentional beings," such as possibles or beings of reason, cannot act, they should not be considered real. By denying intentional being's reality, Father Clarke has been able to make an important distinction in the divine being. The reality attributed to the intentional being possessed by the objects of God's knowledge and love is essentially different from the natural reality of God's infinite *esse*. Thomists can then agree with process metaphysicians to some extent. For, although the divine perfection excludes any mutability in God's natural *esse*, it does not exclude mutability in respect to the objects of God's knowledge and love. God can undergo change in the intentional order, and, because He can, He can be looked on as "really related" to the contingent objects of His love and knowledge.

Although Professor Ford is impressed by the originality and fruitfulness of Norris Clarke's approach to the reality of being, he is not convinced that it provides the answer to his serious objections against divine immutability. The mutability in the intentional objects of God's knowledge and love which Father Clarke is willing to introduce into Thomism does not suffice to ground the type of real relation between God and the world which process metaphysics considers necessary. The being of intentional objects, he observes, is entirely derived from the actual existence of the personal subject who entertains them. But a conscious subject cannot know or love objects unless his consciousness is capable of doing so. And unless the divine consciousness—which, unlike its objects, cannot be distinguished from God's natural existence—were really related to these contingent objects, so that it could be actually affected by them, it is hard to see how the intentional being of the objects known and loved by God could have any grounding. It follows then that, contrary to Father Clarke's contention, the intentional mutability of known and loved objects cannot be reconciled with the natural immutability of the divine existence.

5

Furthermore, as a conscious knower and lover, related to the other beings in the world, God must be a determinate being. He must be *this* rather than *that*. To be determinate in its actuality, excluding other possibilities, a being must be finite; and, as a finite consciousness, God must be capable of enrichment through His knowledge and love of the beings opposed to Him in a finite world. That is why only the *a priori* type of metaphysics—which Kant stigmatized as "dogmatic" because, developed in independence of personal experience, it need not be adequate or applicable to experience—could conceive the perfection of personal consciousness as infinite immutable being.

The notion of being, rather than the notion of perfection, is the major difference between Professor Ford and Father Clarke in their metaphysics of the divine reality. Professor Ford has no desire to deny the divine perfection. In fact, as a theist, he believes that he must affirm it. The Thomists are not wrong, he thinks, in believing that God is perfect. But they are very wrong when they identify the divine perfection with the simple Pure Act of Being. Rather than conceiving God to be the utterly simple perfect being, philosophers should consider Him the perfect instantiation of becoming. Then God could be thought of as everlasting concrescence, the growing together of all things, whether necessary or contingent, within one divine experience. God would no longer be the motionless perfection of unity. He would be the processive perfection of unification. Drawing things ceaselessly into ever greater unity, the divine perfection would be characterized by its unending growth. Such a God, infinite in His potentiality but always finite in His actuality, could neither be, nor could He become, the simple, eternal Pure Act of Being.

Challenging as Father Clarke finds Professor Ford's conception of God as the supreme instantiation of becoming, he cannot bring himself as a Thomist to accept it. Nevertheless, as he tells us in his response to Professor Ford, the objections that process metaphysicians have raised against his philosophy of God and his own personal reflection have moved him to extend the revisions which he had already made in the Thomistic metaphysics of the divine perfection. He would now admit that God is affected in His own inner life by His "extroverted" life of consciousness with respect to creatures. Genuine though that affection is, however, it is restricted to the relative type of affection proper to God's personal relation to creatures. It implies no change in God in any absolute way.

Furthermore, Father Clarke can no longer accept St. Thomas' own position that God's eternal knowledge encompasses the universe of possible and actual beings *as an actually completed infinite multitude* in a single timeless vision. For an infinite multitude, such as the possibles and actuals, *can never be completed*; and a multitude that is *incapable of being completed* cannot be *known as completed* even by the divine mind. The only way out of the contradiction in which St. Thomas has involved himself is to admit that God knows this infinite multitude of beings in the very process of its completion. That admission implies that there must be some kind of eternal "flow" in the objects of God's eternal knowledge. In other words, there must be in God, in a way proper to Himself alone, a spiritual "time" flow. True enough, the eternal now in which God knows the multitude of possibles and actuals is outside our creaturely time and above it. For all of that, however, we must still concede that, in a way peculiar to God Himself, the eternal divine knowledge is spiritually "temporal."

Professor Caputo's essay directs our attention to the finite human person, one of the starting-points of Norris Clarke's "journey of the mind to God." In Professor Ford's essay a number of challenging questions were raised about the divine perfection, the term of that journey. God, Professor Ford proposed, should be identified with perfect becoming rather than with perfect being. Professor Smith's essay, "Two Journeys to the Divine Presence," as its title makes clear, is a critical contemporary reflection on the mind's ascent to God. Father Clarke believes that there are two "paths" to God that

7

complement each other. There is an "inner path" from the human spirit to its Creator and End that focuses on the dynamism of the reflecting subject's intellect and will. There is also an "outer path" from the world on which the mind reflects. This second "path" mounts through causal arguments from the finite contingent beings of the outer world to their infinite creative source.

In his essay Professor Smith re-assesses these two ways to God, the Augustinian and Anselmian "inner way" and the "outer way" associated with Albertus Magnus and Thomas Aquinas. Since the time of Kant, philosophers have commonly identified the inner way with the ontological argument and the outer way with the cosmological argument. To do that, however, Professor Smith argues, is to misunderstand the nature of both the Augustinian and the Thomistic way to God. Far from being "proofs" in the strict sense in which mathematical reasoning can be called a proof, the two "ways" should be more properly considered "journeys" through disciplined reasoning to an intellectual understanding of the God who is present to the believer through the medium of his concrete experience. Once these two "journeys" have been returned to their proper medieval context of "faith seeking understanding," we can see readily enough that they are not as diverse in their starting-point and form of reasoning as some modern theologians—Paul Tillich, for example—believe they are.

The ontological and the cosmological journey to God are two distinct ways of making explicit two different patterns of intelligibility discovered in our religious experience. The Augustinian journey is a rational or dialectical ascent to God and the first principles in terms of which everything is to be understood. The Thomistic way to God, on the other hand, is an inferential journey from a given existent and those of its features which are better known to us. Its terminus is the divine existence, which is not directly available to us apart from an inferential process involving the principle of causality.

This does not mean, however, as Tillich seems to believe,

that the starting-point of Thomas' cosmological journey is a world from which God is "absent," so that the God who is reached at its term is a previously unknown "Stranger." In Kant's understanding of causality, it might be true enough that a causal argument from a finite existent could not terminate at an infinite existent without a *saltus*. The case is quite different, however, in the medieval movement from faith to understanding. For, in that movement, the starting-point is not bare finite existence. Rather it is the divine presence in the contingent cosmos.

Both the ontological and the cosmological arguments are discursive movements from a grasp of the divine presence in a created medium, the mind itself or the cosmos on which the mind reflects, to an explicit, although imperfect, understanding of the transcendent God. It is a mistake then to think, as Tillich seems to do, that Augustine's ontological journey to God is completely *immediate* and *intuitive*, whereas Thomas' cosmological journey is all *inferential* and *demonstrative*. Augustine says very clearly that the knowledge of God acquired through the Neoplatonic ascent of his *De Trinitate* is the conclusion of a dialectical movement involving argument and processes of thought. He also makes it clear that the mind from which the ascent to the Supreme Truth begins is a mutable *medium*, distinct from the Changeless Truth Itself. God is present in the soul according to the measure of its capacity.

Because the mutable mind is the created image in which God is present, the mind's meditative reflection on itself can bring to light the eternal truths, which have always existed within it, and the Uncreated Light through which these truths can be seen. Whatever immediacy of apprehension may be found at the end of this dialectic ascent to Uncreated Truth, it can never be more than a mediated immediacy which Professor Smith compares to the mediated immediacy of Hegel.

The divine presence in the created cosmos is the starting-point of Thomas' cosmological journey to God through Aristotelian causal arguments. For, in Thomas' conception of creation, the transcendent Creator is immanent in the contingent world that is the term of His creative causality. Thus, far from being Tillich's absent "Stranger," encountered for the first time at the term of a causal argument, God is seen to be already immanent in the world as the medium through which He reveals His existence to the religious man's reflective intelligence.

The *divine presence*, then, either in the soul or in the cosmos, is the link that closes the gap between the ontological and the cosmological journeys to God. Contrary to Tillich's contention, the cosmological way to God is not an argument to an "absent God" who *must be*. Both the ontological and cosmological ways set out on their respective journeys from the *presence* in religious experience of the God who *is*. They are diverse because the pattern of intelligibility which each of them makes explicit is different. Yet they are linked together because both of the two patterns of intelligibility, in the mind or in the world, are ways through which the divine presence in our religious experience manifests itself explicitly to the reflective mind.

Professor Smith's two journeys to the divine presence are rather similar to Father Clarke's "inner" and "outer" path to God—a similarity which Father Clarke is very ready to admit. Yet he believes that the similarity could be even closer, if Professor Smith were to temper his criticism of St. Thomas' Aristotelianism. As Professor Smith sees it, Thomas, in his cosmological journey to God, replaced Augustinian *sapientia* with an Aristotelian *scientia* that showed no sign of God's presence in His created world. Norris Clarke is not convinced that Professor Smith's criticism is justified. The dynamism of the mind, which undergirds Aristotelian ascent to God, he claims, is the "natural light" of the mind. In the Thomistic synthesis of Aristotelianism and Neoplatonism the mind's natural dynamism is an in-built participation in the divine light itself. In other words, it is Thomas' Aristotelian reinterpretation of Augustinian illumination theory. For Thomism is not a pure Aristotelianism; it is an Aristotelianism transformed and enriched by Neoplatonic participation metaphysics.

The same participation metaphysics manifests itself in Thomas' account of causality and makes his metaphysics of cause and effect richer and deeper than the account of causality which modern philosophy proposes. For Thomas, the supreme pure act is not just the cause of motion as it is for Aristotle. Thomas' Pure Act of *Esse* is the agent responsible for the very existence of every finite effect. Participating His own reality through His creative efficient causality, God is present in the very being of each finite participant. The modern objection against Thomas' ascent to God—an objection to which Professor Smith seems to show some sympathy—is that from a finite effect a causal argument can reach no further than a finite cause. But once the true nature of Thomas' metaphysics of causality has been understood, that objection against him loses all its force. For Thomas, the human mind can grasp the presence of the transcendent infinite cause immanent in its effect.

Taken together, the three essays in this book challenge Norris Clarke's whole account of the universe as a journey. Professor Caputo questions the starting-point of Father Clarke's philosophy. Can the human subject transcend the ambiguous world of finite beings in which he finds himself to come to Being through a metaphysics of intelligibility, finality, and action? Professor Ford objects to Father Clarke's metaphysics of a transcendent One, identified with infinite Being, as the source and term of the universe's journey. Process metaphysicians simply cannot accept the identification of a personally conscious God with the utterly simple, naturally immutable One, the impassive alpha and omega of a cosmic cycle of activity. And, although he comes quite close to Father Clarke in his critical reflection on the two ways to God, Professor Smith expresses some rather serious reserves about a Thomistic metaphysics of causality in his account of the cosmological journey to the divine presence. Thus, being, intelligibility, action, finality, time, eternity, and unity are among the important elements in Father Clarke's own metaphysics that become topics of lively discussion both in the essays and in Father Clarke's response to them.

In the conversation between Norris Clarke and his three interlocutors about the universe as a journey, the originality and power of his metaphysics comes to light. And, in responding to the three essays published after his Suarez Lecture in this volume, he has taken the opportunity to clarify and, at times, to modify his metaphysics of God and being.

Up to the present, Father Clarke has not given us a single synthetic account of his own metaphysics. His published exposition of it has been confined to the books and to the numerous articles that have been devoted to individual topics. To collect them all in order to make a personal synthesis of Norris Clarke's philosophy requires some time and effort. It occured to the editor then that the reader's profit might be enhanced if a synthetic account of Father Clarke's philosophy, drawn from the *corpus* of his works, were presented at the beginning of this volume. This the editor has endeavored to do in the introductory essay, "An Alert and Independent Thomist: William Norris Clarke, s.j."

GERALD A. McCOOL, s.j.

Fordham University

An Alert and Independent Thomist: William Norris Clarke, S.J.

GERALD A. McCOOL, S.J.

Fordham University

THE EUROPEAN BACKGROUND

IN 1936 NORRIS CLARKE was sent as a young Scholastic to study for his licentiate in philosophy at the Collège Saint Louis on the island of Jersey. There for the next three years, in the philosophate of the Paris Province of the Society of Jesus, he came across the tensions of the Neo-Scholastic movement in the teaching of the remarkable group of Jesuit professors on its faculty. Pedro Descoqs,[1] the passionate defender of Suarez' interpretation of St. Thomas, had little sympathy for his equally distinguished colleague, André Marc.[2] Marc was a Thomist and, in Descoqs' eyes, a Jesuit Thomist was bad enough. Even worse, however, Marc was one of those Jesuit Thomists influenced by the thought of Joseph Maréchal, and Maréchalian Thomism, associated with Kant's subjective starting-point in epistemology, was vigorously opposed by the Suarezians on the Jesuit faculties of philosophy and theology. One reflection of their hostility to anything like a subjective starting-point was the absence of Blondel's *L'Action*[3] from the list of books recommended for reading at the Collège Saint Louis. Recommended or not, however, *L'Action* was read with care and appreciation by the young Scholastics, and, by the time he returned to New York to take his M.A. at Ford-

13

ham, Norris Clarke had mastered it thoroughly. At Fordham, where he wrote his thesis under the mentorship of Anton Pegis, he became well acquainted with the Thomism of Etienne Gilson.

After theological studies and ordination at Woodstock, he returned to Europe in 1947 for two more years of philosophical study. At Louvain, from which he received his Ph.D. in 1949, he encountered again the inner tensions at work in the development of Neo-Thomism.

During the eleven years that had intervened between his arrival at Jersey and his return to Europe, a number of important developments had taken place within the Neo-Thomist movement. One of these was the rediscovery of the central place of the act of existence in St. Thomas' epistemology and metaphysics. The distinguishing characteristic of Thomism, it was now claimed, was its uniqueness as a metaphysics of *esse*. The outcome of this revolutionary shift in the interpretation of St. Thomas—for which, above all others, credit is due to Etienne Gilson—was the emergence of post-war existential Thomism.[4] For the existential Thomists, being was *esse*, the concrete act of existence. The real was the actual existent. It was not intelligible essence as Avicenna thought,[5] and—no matter what Pedro Descoqs might claim—neither was it the possible being of Suarezian metaphysics.[6] Nor was being primarily substance, as Aristotle believed.[7] The Act that made being real and intelligible was not substantial form; it was concrete *esse*.

In that case the intelligibility of being could not be grasped through any sort of conceptual abstraction. Even the third degree of abstraction, favored by Cajetan and John of St. Thomas, was unequal to the task. Being's intelligibility could be grasped through the judgment of existence alone;[8] and its abstraction was really a separation accomplished through the negative judgment distinguishing *esse* from any of its concrete subjects. This meant, of course, that the classical Thomism of the Dominican Commentators, on which Maritain had built his *Degrees of Knowledge*, was no more authentic

Thomism than the metaphysics of Pedro Descoqs' idol, Francis Suarez.

Another important development in Neo-Thomism had been the rediscovery of the important role played by Neoplatonic participation metaphysics in the philosophy of St. Thomas. Cornelio Fabro had called attention to St. Thomas' participation metaphysics in 1939. His pioneering study, *La Nozione metafisica di partecipazione secondo s. Tommaso d'Aquino*,[9] had challenged Gilson's interpretation of St. Thomas as an Aristotelian anti-Platonist. For Gilson, St. Thomas, in opposition to St. Bonaventure, had made the decisive move away from Plato to Aristotle. Thomism therefore was fundamentally opposed to Augustinianism, Bonaventurianism, or any form of Platonism. Because Thomas had sided with Aristotle against Plato, he had been able to guarantee the proper autonomy of created agents in their being, activity, and knowledge.[10] Because Thomas had taken his stand against the Platonic metaphysics of the good proposed by Plotinus, Pseudo-Dionysius, and Eriugena, he had been able to create his Christian philosophy of being.[11]

Gilsonian anti-Platonism was soon challenged by another important study on participation. The well-known Dominican Thomist L.-B. Geiger published his major work, *La Participation dans la philosophie de Saint Thomas d'Aquin* in 1942.[12] The influence of the new interpretation of St. Thomas was soon felt around Europe. At Louvain, the distinguished metaphysician Louis De Raeymaeker recognized the significance of the rediscovery of St. Thomas' participation metaphysics and revised his own metaphysics in the light of it.[13]

The systematic vigor and historical scholarship of the Neo-Thomistic renascence were still in evidence during those early post-war years. At Louvain, De Raeymaeker, Dondeyne, and Van Riet made major contributions to Neo-Thomism's understanding of its own history and to the realization of its speculative possibilities. Among the historians of philosophy on the faculty, Fernand Van Steenberghen—a systematic philosopher in his own right—challenged Gilson's interpretation of St. Bonaventure's Christian philosophy.[14] Through his study of heterodox Aristotelianism and the intellectual movements of the time, Van Steenberghen, in fact, was one of Gilson's more outspoken critics.[15] Thus, although Gilson's metaphysics of *esse* might have received a sympathetic reception at Louvain, his anti-Platonism was rejected by De Raeymaeker and his understanding of Christian philosophy was contested by Van Steenberghen.

Maritain was a stranger to Louvain, and the University faculty had never been particularly friendly to Maréchal. Suarezianism, as a Jesuit invention, was not especially welcome at a University whose relations with the Society of Jesus had not always been cordial. At Louvain, therefore, Father Clarke encountered a Thomism that did not embrace any of the schools with which Americans were familiar during the post-war years. It was neither Maritainian nor Gilsonian. It was not Suarezian. Neither was it transcendental Thomist. Alert, historically and systematically, to all the currents in Thomism, the Thomism of Louvain in the post-war years was independent. That sort of alertness and independence, on the evidence of his own career, must have been congenial to Father Clarke.

CAREER IN AMERICA

In 1949 Norris Clarke was appointed to the pontifical faculty of philosophy at Woodstock, Maryland. The pontifical faculties of philosophy and theology for the Maryland and New York Provinces of the Society of Jesus were located there at that time. When the philosophical faculty was transferred to Bellarmine College, Plattsburgh, New York, Father Clarke went with it and continued to serve as its professor of metaphysics until his appointment to Fordham University in 1955.

From the beginning of his career as a teacher and writer in America, Norris Clarke's publications and his courses in metaphysics, epistemology, medieval philosophy, and philosophy of religion showed the influence of the Maréchalianism, ex-

16

istential Thomism, participationism, and personalism with which he had become acquainted in Europe. Five years of study at two distinguished faculties of philosophy had made him a careful historian of medieval philosophy with a deep respect for the text of St. Thomas. They had also given him the philosophical orientation which he retained through thirty-five years of interaction with other American philosophers. Father Clarke was a Thomist, sympathetic to the leading schools of contemporary Thomism and ready to learn from them, but independent in his approach to all of them.

Maréchalianism had influenced his thinking through André Marc in his student days at Jersey. In the early articles, published relatively soon after his return from Europe, high praise was given to Joseph de Finance's *Être et agir*.[16] Continued openness to the Maréchalian emphasis on the subject was shown through his translation of de Finance's article "Being and Subjectivity" in 1956.[17] The following year the name of Norris Clarke was mentioned among the list of colleagues to whom Bernard Lonergan expressed his thanks in the preface to his *Insight*.[18]

Although Maréchalian Thomism and Gilsonian existential Thomism were generally considered incompatible, Norris Clarke, like de Finance, saw no intrinsic incompatibility between a stress on the personal subject as the starting-point of metaphysics and a focus on the act of existence as the unifying ground of St. Thomas' participation metaphysics. In the philosophy of St. Thomas, God, as Infinite *Esse*, the pure act of existence, was a free and consciously active person. God's expansive generosity as Infinite Good, the unitary active source through whose causality being was communicated, was the creative ground of a finite community of subsisting agents. Active communication of existence by their free, intelligent Creator endowed the multiplicity of finite existents with their own power of active self-communication. At being's highest created level, on which finite existents shared in their Creator's free self-possession, the community of interacting beings was a community of interacting persons. Each personal agent imitated the expansive goodness of its unitary source by sharing its own reality with the other members of its community. At the same time, however, each conscious agent retained its personal identity through its dynamic self-possession as an intelligent free subject.

In this metaphysics of creative participation, the starting-point of philosophical reflection should not be restricted to reflection by an isolated subject on the conditions of possibility for its own thought. A reflection adequate to full self-awareness must include a reflection on the implications of experience of a personal agent in a community of interacting persons.[19] From this it followed that Marcel's criticism of Descartes was justified. Philosophy should not begin with the implications of a Cartesian "I think." Rather it should begin with the dynamic "we are" of a community of personal agents who reveal themselves to each other through their action. Reflection on interpersonal experience, Norris Clarke believed, opened the way to a participation metaphysics of action and creation that could incorporate the insights of Maréchalian and existential Thomism into a richer and more authentic Thomistic synthesis. At the same time it distinguished his own epistemology both from the epistemology of Maréchal and Lonergan, whose starting-point was the dynamism of the isolated subject, and, on the other hand, from the epistemology of Gilson and Maritain, whose starting-point was the objective judgment of sense experience.

A number of articles, published soon after Father Clarke's return from Europe, were devoted to the implications of St. Thomas' metaphysics of participation.[20] Fairly soon, they were followed by the brief but revolutionary essay "What Is Really Real?" in which, committing himself to a radically existential Thomism, he argued against the Suarezians and traditional Thomists that possible being, since it was incapable of action, had no title to reality.[21] Through these early publications, several essential elements of his own metaphysics—existence, participation, interaction—were defended as authentic characteristics of St. Thomas' own thought.

Later in his career Norris Clarke engaged in a protracted dialogue with American philosophy. Personal experience of the East and his work as editor of the *International Philosophical Quarterly* stimulated his interest in Oriental metaphysics and philosophy of religion. One of the results of these new interests was a fruitful encounter between his own metaphysics of existence, action, and person with American process philosophy. Another was an equally fruitful dialogue with American linguistic philosophy on the nature and validity of the human person's knowledge of God through analogous language. A third was a stimulating reflection on the philosophy of the self in Eastern and Western thought.[22]

Building upon his experience of European Thomism, Father Clarke worked out a nuanced, yet highly coherent, metaphysics in his thirty-five years of teaching and writing in America. It was a Thomism deeply respectful of St. Thomas' own text, yet fearlessly original in its personal development of basic Thomistic insights. In his own philosophy, Norris Clarke felt no compunction in parting company with St. Thomas' own teaching—as he did, for example, in his proofs for God's existence—when another approach recommended itself as sounder and more in keeping with St. Thomas' own principles.[23]

In tracing the development of Norris Clarke's metaphysics through its earlier and later stages we are struck with its originality, consistency, and power. Even from a purely historical point of view, in fact, retracing his career can be quite instructive. His teaching career overlapped the career of Bernard Lonergan and the major part of Karl Rahner's intellectual activity. Outstanding representatives of St. Thomas' inspiration though they were, Lonergan and Rahner were both theologians. No Thomist, to my knowledge, who has devoted himself to purely philosophical activity has retained without interruption a position of distinction as Father Clarke has from 1950 to the present. In that respect, his status as a contemporary representative of the Thomistic tradition is unique. Nevertheless, we can observe in his philosophical development an evolution not unlike the evolution that occurred in the Thomism of Lonergan and Rahner. Like these Thomist theologians, he has lived through the transition from the Thomism of the ecclesiastical faculties to the Thomism of the university. Like them, he has experienced the change from a Thomism marked by its fidelity to one or other of the doctrinal schools to a Thomism of personal philosophical commitment. As an historian of philosophy, Father Clarke has always been very conscious of his responsibility to the text. As a creative philosopher, on the other hand, his only responsibility has been to himself and to the truth. For him, to be a Thomist is not to be a member of a school; it is to philosophize freely and responsibly in the light of a great tradition.

A METAPHYSICS OF THE ACTING PERSON

Through his early publications on participation, Norris Clarke began to work out his own dynamic metaphysics of the acting person. God was the supreme intelligible and the highest Good because He was the Infinite Pure Act of *Esse*. In his own philosophy of being, St. Thomas had transformed Plotinus' metaphysics of the good into his own metaphysics of being and creation. By doing that, Thomas had also transformed his Aristotelian metaphysics of potency and act from a metaphysics of change to a Platonically inspired participation metaphysics. The act of existence was the ultimate perfection conferred on each creature through God's efficient causality. Concrete essence was the receptive principle limiting the perfection that made it real. This transformation, Father Clarke argued, was one of St. Thomas' great contributions to Western metaphysics.[24] *Esse*, the perfection shared by the multitude of finite existents, was not only the abiding effect of God's creative action; it was itself the dynamic source of every finite being's own activity. That is why, in his controversial essay "What Is Really Real?," Norris Clarke argued that the possibles that had no act of existence of their own must lack reality because they were incapable of action.[25]

Final causality was as important as formal, material, and efficient causality in St. Thomas' transformed metaphysics of emanation and return. In a Plotinian universe the infinite Good was not only the dynamic source from which all finite beings took their origin; the Good was also the infinite Goal to which every finite being endeavored to return through its own activity.[26] For St. Thomas, to act meant to tend toward God. Moved by the love of its Creator, present within it and grounding its finite *esse* by His creative causality, each finite agent strove to "become like God," to participate as fully as possible in the goodness of Infinite *Esse*.

In the early years of this century, a brilliant young Thomist theologian, Pierre Rousselot, had called attention to St. Thomas' Platonic metaphysics of emanation and return and linked it to the dynamic drive of finite thought and love.[27] Aware of itself intuitively, through its non-conceptual act of *intellectus*, the human mind, in Rousselot's interpretation of St. Thomas, was moved to its acts of discursive conceptual knowledge by its innate drive to share in God's reality through the culminating intuition of the Beatific Vision. St. Thomas' philosophy of knowledge, Rousselot claimed, was not the deductive rationalism of the great post-Cartesian philosophers, whose ideal was a tightly locked system of static concepts. On the contrary, St. Thomas' epistemology was an intellectualism. Its ideal was the intuitive self-knowledge of the angel or the soul's intuitive grasp of God through the Beatific Vision. For St. Thomas, in fact, Rousselot continued, no static concept of itself could guarantee the mind's hold on being. Being was grasped through the judgment, whose own truth was guaranteed by the mind's implicit awareness of its innate drive to God's infinite reality. In other words, to use Rousselot's celebrated phrase, "the intellect was the faculty of the real because it was the faculty of the divine."[28]

The heritage of Rousselot was preserved and developed by Maréchal, de Lubac, de Finance, Rahner, and Lonergan. It became the Transcendental Thomist tradition in which the subject's implicit awareness of the knowing and willing activity of his own spirit provides the critical justification for a realistic metaphysics. In this tradition, as we have seen, the dynamic human subject's self-reflection is linked to a participation metaphysics of emanation and return. This was a tradition with which Father Clarke had been familiar and with which he had remained in sympathetic contact. It is no surprise then that, in his courses at Fordham and in his later publications, he was more than willing to draw upon the resources which it offered. Sympathy, however, need not mean discipleship; and, in a number of important points, Father Clarke's critical grounding of his metaphysics differs clearly from the justification proposed by Transcendental Thomists.

COMPARISON WITH TRANSCENDENTAL THOMISM

For Norris Clarke, in opposition to Maréchal and Lonergan, the starting-point of metaphysics must be a reflection on human subjects actively engaged, through dialogue, in the process of mutual self-communication. In that reflection there can be no "bracketing"—even methodologically—of the other person. Through its disciplined use of concepts, reflection makes explicit the richer, if less precise, knowledge of the self already possessed through the non-conceptual act of intuitive *intellectus*. Like Rousselot's Thomism, Father Clarke's critically grounded metaphysics is an intellectualism in which more is always known through *intellectus* than can be enclosed in the sharply defined concepts of discursive *ratio*. For its judgments to be adequate to the rich fullness of self-knowledge, their concepts must be "read in the light" of *intellectus*, the non-conceptual knowledge which surrounds them. The reader who overlooks that fact will fail to see the force of much of Norris Clarke's metaphysical reflection. He will not be able, for example, to see the cogency of Father Clarke's defense of analogous knowledge in his philosophy of God, and the force of Father Clarke's argument for the abiding personal subject, against process philosophy, may escape him. In these, as in many of the most significant reflections in Father

Clarke's metaphysics, immediate grasp of interpersonal experience through *intellectus* provides the evidence for his position.

That is why it is most important to observe that the experience on which Norris Clarke reflects is not simply personal experience but interpersonal experience.[29] For this is an experience from which the active presence of the other cannot be methodologically excluded. In the experience of mutual self-communication, immanent and transient action, even though known only implicitly, reveal their reality immediately. It is through a lived response to a world in which dialogue constantly occurs that the knower becomes aware of the infinite goal of the drive that ceaselessly moves him to learn more about the world's constituents. *Intellectus*, therefore, tells Norris Clarke, as it told Pierre Rousselot, that his infinitely questing mind is the faculty of the real because it is the faculty of the divine. But simultaneously—in time and nature—*intellectus* tells him that his mind is the faculty of the real because it grasps another finite person immediately in dialogue.[30] It follows, then, that action, finality, and being are given immediately, though implicitly, in the experience of a human subject. For his questions reach out to the infinite and their answers are formulated in a language shared with other acting persons. Being, given immediately in experience, is more than simply a transcendental condition of possibility for experience. Father Clarke is an immediate, though reflective, realist. He is not a Transcendental Thomist.

Nevertheless, as opposed to Gilson and Maritain, his realism is grounded immediately upon the free person. For, once reflection on interpersonal experience has been made attentively, it confronts the human subject with a number of vital questions. Is he really in contact with another human subject? Is genuine self-communication of being taking place between them? Is the unlimited desire for knowledge and goodness which he experiences an intelligible movement toward a real goal; or is it no more than an absurd quest for the unattainable? Deductive logic cannot provide the answer to these questions. For they challenge the very intelligibility of being, and the intelligibility of being cannot be derived from the logical principle of contradiction.[31]

Every human knower must answer these questions for himself. He must take upon his own shoulders the accountability for the free and intelligent stand which he adopts to the world in which he already finds himself. Is this world of questions, gestures, signs, and inherited language an intelligible universe of being? Whether his answer be yes or no, it remains a personal option. Should his answer be yes, it is a lived commitment to the principle of intelligibility, the principle on which every realistic metaphysics must rest. Intellectually justified but freely made, an affirmative response is an act of free certitude through which the responsible subject commits himself in thought and action to the intelligibility of being.[32]

THE EXISTENCE OF GOD

In every free intelligent agent, whose activity is sustained by God's own concurring action, there is an in-built drive of intellect and will to the infinite *Esse* of which the agent is a created likeness. This, after all, is a demand of St. Thomas' Platonic metaphysics of participated existence, emanation, and return. Confirmation of its truth, Norris Clarke believes, can be found in the history of religious experience. History of religion, in the East and West, gives evidence of this dynamic drive toward the transcendent in every human heart. It gives testimony as well to the human spirit's intuitive awareness of the transcendent source of its being working within it. Although transcendent, this dynamic source and term of human activity cannot be "totally other." For knowledge and love require a similitude, even if it be a defective one, between the finite agent and the transcendent object of these acts.

God's immanence within the conscious human spirit, as the efficient cause of the in-built drive to know and love, of which He is the transcendent term, is the natural root of religious experience.[33] For that reason, Father Clarke believes, the hu-

24

man spirit's implicit awareness of God's presence within it as
its efficient and final cause can also provide the starting-point
for a philosophical reflection that justifies a reasonable assent
to God's existence.

It should not be a modern representation of St. Thomas'
own Five Ways. For Father Clarke does not find the Five
Ways very useful to the contemporary philosopher. One of
them, in fact, the Third, he considers seriously flawed by a
logical fallacy.[34] Neither should it be a rigidly logical demonstration in the tradition of the great rationalist philosophers.
Its goal is not Cartesian mathematical certitude. Its aim, on
the contrary, is at once more modest and more reasonable.
No more is intended than to justify an assent to God's existence through the reasonable personal commitment which the
Thomists call free certitude.[35]

Drawing on the resources of St. Thomas' own metaphysics,
Norris Clarke's reflection follows a double path. An outward
path considers the finite beings of the surrounding world. An
inner path focuses on the dynamism of the reflecting subject's
intellect and will. Whichever path the reflection follows, its
conclusion is the same. There must exist a unique transcendent source of all beings. Immanent and transcendent at once,
this dynamic originating source works intimately within the
finite beings of the world as their ultimate ground and efficient cause. As the ultimate good in which all finite beings
participate, this source is also the world's final cause, drawing
all finite beings toward itself.[36]

Leading his readers along both paths through a series of
causal arguments, Father Clarke ascends from the many beings
in the world to their unitary source and from the finite beings
in the world to their infinite originating ground.[37] The twofold reflection that leads to God, as Father Clarke presents it,
carries forward the quest for the meaning of interpersonal
experience that should already have led his reader to commit
himself to the principle of intelligibility. If being is intelligible, it must have an intelligible ground. What, then, is the
ground of finite beings, the finite minds which know them,

and of the intelligible relationship between minds and being? Once the natural act of faith in being's intelligibility has been placed, the reflecting subject knows that human minds really act and that their cognitive activity, besides having a real object, has a real goal. But an intelligible striving for intelligibility and goodness whose goal has shown itself to be infinite cannot have its intelligible ground either in the finite beings of the world or in the finite minds which know them. If man is not absurd and the world of being is intelligible, there must be one infinite intelligible ground of both. If the principle of intelligibility is justified, then God exists. Once more we have returned to Father Clarke's great operative principle: the intelligibility of the free reflecting person and of his interaction with his world.

THE ANALOGY OF BEING

Knowledge and love of the world's transcendent ground, Norris Clarke argues, is the in-built goal of the personal agent's spiritual activity. Since "like is known by like," as Plato, Plotinus, and St. Thomas saw so clearly, the transcendent ground and goal of man's spiritual activity therefore cannot be the "totally other."[38] Nevertheless, no specific or generic similitude between finite and infinite is possible. That is why St. Thomas' participation metaphysics calls for a similitude between them in which their whole reality is simultaneously like and unlike. This is the imperfect ontological similitude between the one and the many in St. Thomas' participation metaphysics that grounds the conceptual analogy of being.

The analogy between God and creature, however, is not an analogy of proper proportionality, as Cajetan and the Thomist tradition after him had claimed.[39] According to Cajetan, the likeness between God and creatures is a proportional one: a similarity among sets of relations. The relation between God's essence and His existence or action is imperfectly like the relation between each finite essence and its own existence or action. Apart from this relationship, no likeness is claimed to exist between infinite and finite essences or infinite and finite existences or actions.

Because of his real distinction between essence and existence, St. Thomas could use the analogy of proper proportionality. He was not forced to resort to the Aristotelian analogy of attribution, as Francis Suarez had been. This indeed was fortunate, the Thomists claimed. For the analogy of attribution, based on the cause–effect relation, cannot account for an intrinsic similitude between God and creatures. Color may be related to health as its effect and medicine may be related to it as its cause. But this does not imply that either color or medicine possesses health intrinsically. In Norris Clarke's student days at the Collège Saint Louis when Pedro Descoqs was teaching there, the analogy of being was a hotly debated issue. Thomists and Suarezians both claimed the authority of St. Thomas for their conflicting understandings of its nature.

Historical research by Lyttkens,[40] Montagnes,[41] and Klubertanz,[42] and his own familiarity with the text of St. Thomas, undermined Father Clarke's confidence in Cajetan's interpretation of St. Thomas. St. Thomas had indeed used the analogy of proper proportionality in his early works, but he had soon abandoned it. After a number of shifts, not always mutually compatible, he finally settled on an analogy of causal participation, which combined the analogy of attribution and the analogy of proper proportionality in a single synthesis. This analogy did justice both to the proportional similarity of acts of existence diversified by their varied essences and to the intrinsic similitude between finite participants and the Infinite Final and Efficient Cause to which they were dynamically related as their transcendent source and goal.[43]

As a systematic philosopher, Norris Clarke also came to realize that the analogy of proper proportionality, when used alone, was of little service to the philosopher of God. What could a purely formal rule, informing us that the relation between essence and activity was proportionally similar in God and creatures, tell us about what actions like knowing and loving in God might be when—apart from the rule—God's essence and action remained utterly unknown? Father Clarke could sympathize with the linguistic philosophers who complained that the analogy of proper proportionality, even if it were true, was trivial.[44] He was convinced, however, that the same complaint could not be made about St. Thomas' analogy of causal participation.

In a series of significant essays, Norris Clarke drew on the resources of his own metaphysics of being, action, and participation to counter the challenge of linguistic philosophy to the meaningfulness of God-talk.[45] When concepts are moved heedlessly from one language game into another, the linguistic philosophers observe, their meaning can be considerably altered. A philosopher can make that sort of linguistic shift without adverting to what he is doing. The result is that he begins to talk nonsense.

God-talk can entail that sort of nonsense. Concepts denoting sense objects, human cognition, or emotion are meaningful enough in the context of intra-worldly discourse. When they are shifted, without fair warning, into a new and strange language game in which the subject to which they are applied is an infinite extra-worldly being, the linguistic situation becomes quite different. In their new context, where they function in a completely different way, their meaning becomes extremely hard to specify. In fact, since they no longer refer to a designable intra-worldly object of experience, what, if anything, such concepts mean is an open question. Analogous language used of God may be nonsense, for all we know; and, if theists wish to use it, they must justify its meaningfulness before they do so.

Norris Clarke is more than willing to meet the challenge. His appeal once more is to the natural roots of religious experience. These roots, as we recall, are the human spirit's

28

intuitive awareness of God's active presence and of its own ceaseless drive in knowledge and love to a transcendent object that must be, in some way, like it.[46] This experience, known through *intellectus*, played an important part in Father Clarke's argument for God's existence. It plays an equally important role in his justification of analogous language about God.

Present through His activity in the human spirit, God is not the "totally other"—an unknown being without relationship to man or to the world. On the contrary, as the only intelligible ground for the world's existence—its cause in the authentic metaphysical sense of that term—He is present in the world while transcending it.[47] God can be known, then, by mounting from the realities encountered in the world through the classic triple way: affirming finite realities, negating their limitations, and raising their perfection to an infinite degree. For Father Clarke, therefore, defense of analogous language used of God is built upon a realistic causal metaphysics of creation and participation, emanation and return.

The concepts in which analogous knowledge of God is expressed are open-ended and systematically vague. Some are open-ended at both ends—they have neither "ceiling" nor "floor,"[48] as Norris Clarke puts it: i.e., they are applicable throughout the whole range of being, from the highest to the lowest, as, for example, being, activity, unity, intelligibility, goodness. Others are open-ended at the top but not at the bottom (they have no "ceiling" but they do have a "floor"): i.e., they are not applicable below a certain level of being, as, for example, intelligence, life, freedom, personality, love. But in both cases, concepts applicable to God must be open-ended at the top. For perfections that are unlimited in their very nature can transcend every finite mode of intra-worldly instantiation. Concepts representing them can "stretch their meaning" to embrace infinite instantiation in the infinite source of the finite world. How the perfections they represent manifest themselves in that transcendent source, they themselves, as limited human concepts, cannot reveal. Vague and open-ended, as they must be, they elude all attempts to pin them down to sharp, positive definition.[49]

This does not mean, however, that analogous concepts are devoid of meaning. In their lived use in human judgments, vague as they are, these concepts preserve an identifiable unity of meaning as they move from one linguistic context to another. As they shift, in lived human experience from one language game to another, they "stretch their meaning," as expanding heuristic concepts, to embrace the similarities which the human mind discovers in the interrelated objects of its universe of being.

For, once assent has been given to being's intelligibility through the natural act of faith, the human knower is aware that the real beings which he encounters in his experience possess the power of active presence. Since each of them, through its active presence, can partially satisfy the boundless desire of his spirit to know and love, each of these beings, related to one another in an intelligible world of unity and multiplicity, must possess, in its own unique way, the transcendental attributes of unity, intelligibility, and goodness. And so, Father Clarke declares, the human mind is engaged, from the very beginning of its intellectual life, in a necessary co-involvement with being, intelligibility, and analogy.[50]

The dissatisfaction, which the mind experiences with the limit imposed upon its drive by any finite object, moves it to transcend all limits and to strive to know the infinite. How precisely that infinite being will manifest the absolutely transcendental attributes of unity, intelligibility, power, activity, and goodness, the finite inquiring mind cannot know. But it does understand that, as the object of the same desire, the infinite must be *like* the finite beings which the mind already knows in its possession of these absolutely transcendental attributes.[51]

In similar manner, the dissatisfaction of the human will with the limited goods which it has attained or still intends points it beyond the finite world to a being of limitless goodness and value. Limited and unsatisfying as they are in their finite instantiations, there are values which demand the personal agent's unconditional approval. They manifest themselves as perfections which he judges absolutely better to have than not to have. Once these pure perfections have been freed from their finite limitations, they can be projected upward upon an open-ended scale and affirmed of the infinite source in whose truth and goodness all finite values participate. Such are the pure perfections which Norris Clarke considers relatively transcendental properties legitimately affirmed of God. Among them can be listed knowledge, consciousness, love, joy, happiness, and similar properties of personality in the widest possible sense.[52]

Urged on by the restless drive of his spiritual dynamism, the human knower is impelled constantly to expand the horizon of his knowledge and, as he does so, to thematize his discoveries through the open-ended heuristic concepts of his analogous discourse. Analogy as such does not extend human knowledge. The drive of the mind does that. Analogy enables the knower to unify and organize his expanded knowledge when it is acquired.[53]

Thus it is the drive of the finite spirit, intuitively grasped by *intellectus*, which enables the analogous concepts of discursive *ratio* to preserve their unity while they "stretch their meaning" to adjust to the mounting levels of intelligibility through which the mind passes on its ascent to God. Intuitive awareness of its own restless movement becomes the intelligent "pointer" that enables the mind to understand, in a flash of intuitive insight, that, infinitely different from them as it must be, the transcendent source of the finite perfections that fail to satisfy its drive to know and love must still be in some way like them. Intuitive insight, therefore, guarantees the "shift in meaning" which open-ended heuristic concepts undergo when they are used in the living language game of God-talk. If that be true, as Father Clarke contends, the attempt of some distinguished Thomists to vindicate the meaningful employment of analogous concepts through an analysis of analogy's logical structure alone cannot succeed.[54] Without a careful reflection on man's lived experience, cognitive, affective, and religious, the restless movement penetrated by his natural desire for the transcendent infinite operating within it, the intelligent justification of meaningful analogous discourse about God will not manifest itself.[55]

That is why the Thomist should resolutely reject the demand of linguistic philosophers that God's definition be specified clearly in advance of any effort to establish God's existence. For, in Father Clarke's realistic metaphysics, God's transcendental attributes emerge from the same ascending movement of the mind that establishes God's existence.[56] The Thomist metaphysician does not start out "to prove God's existence." On the contrary, committing himself to the intelligibility of being through his act of natural faith, he draws upon the resources of his whole conscious experience in a persistent quest for the intelligible ground of his own activity and of the world with which he interacts.

DIALOGUE WITH PROCESS PHILOSOPHY

As a metaphysician with a keen interest in philosophy of religion, Norris Clarke had a natural sympathy for Whitehead's process philosophy, and many of his good friends were found among its adherents. For all of that, he was never tempted to become a Whiteheadian himself. There are too many fundamental differences between his own metaphysics and Whiteheadian metaphysics for that to be possible. Norris Clarke's metaphysics is a Thomistic metaphysics built upon the act of existence. Its God, Infinite Existence, grounded the multiplicity of contingent finite existents through His creative efficient causality. No finite reality could be *causa sui*, as Whitehead's creativity was claimed to be. As the unique self-grounding ground of a contingent multiplicity, therefore, Norris Clarke's God was very different from the God of Whitehead's metaphysics, the finite supreme instantiation of self-grounding creativity. The relation between the grounding one and the grounded many in Norris Clarke's metaphysics is asymmetrical. God could act on creatures, but creatures could not act on God. This makes Norris Clarke's God what Whitehead claimed God could never be, the supreme exception in the universe. Known only indirectly through analogy, God transcended the finite multitude who needed Him but of which He had no need.

Even on the finite level there were fundamental differences between Norris Clarke's metaphysics and Whitehead's metaphysics. In Father Clarke's metaphysics, for example, action—the key to his realistic philosophy of being—does not "come from behind" as it did in Whitehead's process metaphysics. Action and passion were always simultaneous. And, above all, whereas substance was the Whiteheadians' *bête noire*, Norris Clarke believes that Thomism's dynamic metaphysics of substance is one of its greatest contributions to contemporary philosophy.[57]

St. Thomas' substance, he insisted, should not be confused with the inert substance of Descartes and Locke, which Whitehead had rightly criticized. Far from being the unknowable substrate of accidents, as Locke's inert substance had been, St. Thomas' substance manifested itself to human consciousness as the dynamic intelligible ground of the personal identity that perdured through the personal agent's intellectual and moral activity. Far from being inert, substance—united with its accidents to form one complete subsisting being—was a dynamic source and recipient of change. It both changed itself and was changed by others. The perduring identity of personal agents through their mutual communication of being in the process of dialogue was evidence of that. Properly understood, Norris Clarke maintained, the dynamic Thomistic metaphysics of substance was more adequate to the intellectual and moral experience of the human person than the Whiteheadian metaphysics of the "atomic" actual entity.

Nevertheless, despite the differences between them, Whiteheadians could still teach Thomists a thing or two. Norris Clarke was quite convinced of that, and two of the most interesting modifications which he believes should be made in contemporary Thomism were suggested to him by his contact with process metaphysics.

The first is an extensive overhaul of its Aristotelian metaphysics of relations. In its reaction against the Cartesian metaphysics of the isolated, self-sufficient substance, Whiteheadian metaphysics emphasized the interrelatedness of the actual entities in our universe. In Whiteheadian process philosophy, every actual entity is influenced in its concrescence by every other actual entity in the world which it prehends. Interrelatedness, in fact, was one of the most cogent reasons for Whitehead's decision to substitute a metaphysics of processive, prehending actual entities for a metaphysics of static and self-sufficient substances. In his own metaphysics of actual entities, to be meant to be in relation.

As Father Clarke sees it, Whitehead was partly right. True enough, in St. Thomas' metaphysics, substance was dynamic, not static. Nevertheless, the Angelic Doctor's commitment to the Aristotelian metaphysics of predicamental relations left the dynamic substance of his own metaphysics far too isolated and self-sufficient to do justice to our contemporary knowledge of nature and society.

St. Thomas' predicamental relation—the Aristotelian πρός τι—was no more than an accident inhering in the individual substance. For two things to be related to one another, therefore, each related substance must possess its own accidental πρός τι. The effect of this Aristotelian metaphysics of relations was to reduce the dynamic order of the finite beings in our universe to the sum of the accidental relations inhering in the individual finite substances. For that reason, Father Clarke believes, unless Thomism's metaphysics of relations is radically modified, it cannot do justice to the world of our contemporary experience. For, in that world, dynamic substances do not live in self-sufficient isolation. They exist as members of a system. Far from being related to other substances in a purely accidental way, each substance, in some way or other, is intrinsically constituted by its relation to a system that integrates the individuals within it into a higher unity. Lower systems are incorporated into higher systems, making our universe a system of systems.

Thus, although each substance retains its subsisting identity, its relation to the system in which it exists can enter into its essential constitution. To be a substance therefore means to be a nodal center of actions and relations which Aristotle's metaphysics of substance and πρός τι can no longer handle. Thomists must admit that fact and adapt their metaphysics of relations to integrate the reality of system into their category scheme.[58]

The second modification which Father Clarke suggests for contemporary Thomism is a revised metaphysics of God's immutability and of God's relation to the world. The eternal, impassively immutable God of Thomism has been severely criticized by philosophers in the Whiteheadian tradition, Charles Hartshorne for example. How can a changeless God, unaffected by human action, untroubled by sin, unmoved by prayer, receiving nothing from our devoted service, be the personal, provident God of biblical revelation? Whiteheadians, of course, are not the only ones who object to St. Thomas' philosophy of God; Hegelians have their problems with it too. Nor is Father Clarke the only Thomist to modify his own philosophy of God in order to take account of the objections brought against it. Karl Rahner, to mention one celebrated example, has argued that the infinite God of creation and redemption, though immutable in His own reality, can undergo change "in His other," the finite world in which he "expresses Himself" through His natural and supernatural causality.[59]

Norris Clarke's dialogue, however, has been with Whiteheadian process metaphysics and, in his endeavor to meet its difficulties, his own philosophy of God has evolved progressively in the last decade-and-a-half.

In 1973, in his essay "A New Look at the Immutability of God,"[60] he resorted to the distinction between real and intentional being which he had established in "What Is Really

Real?"[61] The being enjoyed in consciousness by the objects of knowledge and love was intentional being; it was not the real being of the actual existent. It followed then that, in the philosophy of God, a distinction should be made between the purely intentional being which the objects of God's love and knowledge enjoyed in His consciousness and the real being of the infinite existence with which God's essence was identified. Even though God's real being could never change, the intentional objects of His consciousness would vary, depending upon God's free choice to create or not to create a finite world. Furthermore, although God's real being could not be affected by the action of His creatures, the intentional being of the objects known and loved by God would vary according to the free choices made by saints and sinners. The provident love of a personal God would have to "vary," in its own timeless way, in order to respond as it should to the acts, vice and virtue, which mark the historical course of a human life. Thomists were right enough in saying that a God whose infinitely simple *esse* could undergo no physical change could not be really related to the world. But they had by no means said all that they should have said. For an infinite person, whom creatures could affect in the intentional being of His consciousness, must also be considered intentionally related to the world. Thomists therefore should insist that the provident God of their metaphysics is truly, though *personally*, related to the world. Mutable, as He was, in the intentional order, St. Thomas' God was indeed the God of biblical revelation.

By 1979, however, the year in which his *The Philosophical Approach to God* was published, Norris Clarke still believed that what he had said in 1973 was technically defensible. Nevertheless, he no longer considered it an adequate response to process metaphysics.[62] It would be more profitable, he now thought, simply to drop the distinction between real and personal relations. Thomists should honestly admit that, in some aspects of His being at least, God is really related to the world. The old doctrine was true in the older, more restrictive context of Aristotelian metaphysics. But, once the metaphysician has made the option to work within the less restrictive contemporary context in which the order of the person and interpersonal relations have become the prime analogue for the concepts used in his metaphysics, another and "looser" meaning for "real relation" is called for. The free person, rather than the impersonal nature of Aristotelian physics, has now become the model from which the fundamental concepts of our philosophy are drawn.[63]

In that new context, it is no longer difficult for a Thomist to admit that a mutual giving and receiving of personal love takes place between God and creature, and that God's consciousness becomes contingently and qualitatively different because of it. This difference, however, is restricted to the relational level of God's consciousness. It in no way implies any increase in the ontological perfection of God's intrinsic inner being, or what St. Thomas would call the absolute, as opposed to the relational, aspect of God's being. Thomists should have no fear that admitting such contingent relational change in God would jeopardize God's infinite perfection. For, as we understand today, to give and receive love is a sign of perfection rather than of imperfection in a personal agent.[64] Thomists' admission of conscious relational change in God, therefore, no longer implies the compromising of any really essential principles. They can even go so far as to admit that such change is temporal, as long as they understand that "God's time" is of an incomprehensibly different modality from the time of our contingent, moving world.[65]

The whole quarrel over God's immutability can now be laid to rest. All the Thomist need say today is that some kinds of change can be considered appropriate for an infinitely perfect person, while other kinds cannot.

Despite these gracious concessions, Norris Clarke's position in 1979 did not seem to differ fundamentally from the one which he defended in 1973, except for its willingness to tolerate—without great enthusiasm—some sort of temporal change in God. His fellow Thomists might well observe that both positions still rested upon Father Clarke's distinction between real and intentional being. Although God's conscious relation to the world was now called "real" rather than personal, its intentional "reality" was of a very different nature from the actual reality of God's absolutely existing essence. Father Clarke's revised metaphysics of God's immutability still seemed to rest on a distinction which many of his fellow Thomists would not permit him to make. Joseph Maréchal most certainly would not. For the reality of intentional being is the foundation on which Maréchal's Transcendental Thomism is built.[66]

AN ORIGINAL METAPHYSICS OF ACT AND POTENCY

From the early articles, published soon after his return from Europe, Norris Clarke's commitment to the metaphysics of act and potency was clear, and, through the course of his long career, it has been unwavering. In those early articles, limitation of the act of existence by a potential principle of limitation was an essential element in his metaphysics of creation and participation, and, in an important article, published after a quarter-century of teaching, the dynamic metaphysics of substance and substantial potency was listed among the most relevant elements of St. Thomas' philosophy today.[67]

The same article revealed, however, the extent to which Norris Clarke's metaphysics of act and potency had evolved through his own meditation on the text of St. Thomas and his prolonged contact with contemporary philosophy and science. In its developed form, his metaphysics of act and potency had been transformed into an original synthesis. His fellow Thomists might admire it, but not all of them would agree with it.[68]

For one thing, although Father Clarke remains committed to his metaphysics of diverse participation in existence through the varied limiting modes of essence, he has become very reluctant to speak of a real distinction between the act of existence and essence as its limiting principle. Although a real metaphysical distinction between these two principles of being had been considered a hallmark of Neo-Thomism, Father Clarke no longer thinks it wise for Thomists to insist on it. To speak of its "real" distinction from existence implies that essence is in some way a positive principle in its own right. Yet the one source of all positive reality is existence. Granted that some objective irreducibility is found in the real order between a real perfection and the mode that limits it, Thomists should admit that human concepts cannot grasp more closely what a limit's reality truly is. They would be well advised, then, simply to speak of a real limited participation in existence through essence as its limiting mode, and abandon the effort to determine more closely in what the "reality" of the "composition" between essence and existence consists.[69]

For many Thomists, Norris Clarke's proposal is far from a modest one. At first glance, it appears to compromise the reality of the transcendental relation between essence and existence—one of Neo-Thomism's cardinal principles. It was one thing for Father Clarke to deny the reality of intentional being as a requirement of his existential Thomism, as he had done in "What Is Really Real?" But it would be quite another to water down Thomism's real transcendental relation between essence and existence, as he now appeared to be doing. No wonder, then, that other distinguished Thomists, like Cornelio Fabro and Joseph Owens, reacted unfavorably to anything like this revised metaphysics of essence and existence.[70]

For Father Clarke the metaphysics of act and potency remains as relevant for the metaphysics of change as it does for a metaphysics of participation. Without a dynamic metaphysics of substance and accident the perduring personal identity of the human agent through the interpersonal process of dialogue would not be intelligible, and, to make sense of the deeper level of change—which Thomists call substantial change—a metaphysics of act and potency is still required.

Physics has shown the inadequacy of Cartesian mechanism,

which reduced the larger wholes of the physical world to aggregates of discrete atomic actualities, and philosophers, like Ivor Leclerc, have pointed to potency's indispensable role as a condition of possibility for any complex whole that is not an aggregate. In quantum physics, a potential of some sort is required in order to make sense out of the behavior of subatomic particles. In our contemporary world, therefore, a metaphysics of potency as the subject of continuity in change, possessing the real inner aptitude or capacity to take on some new mode of being and form an intrinsic unity with it, is very much in place. Scientists and philosophers are ready again to recognize the truth of St. Thomas' principle that, in the physical world, an intrinsic unity cannot be made out of two entities in act.[71]

That should not be taken to mean, however, that Norris Clarke would recommend a return to the Thomistic metaphysics of substantial form and primary matter as Thomists have understood it in the past. The basic structure of that act–potency relationship remains quite sound but, once again, some revision will be required to make it adequate to the data of contemporary science.

The intrinsic unity of complex wholes is of a higher order than the unity of merely accidental aggregates. Complex wholes are genuine *una per se*. In the living body, for example, lower components, like molecules and cells, although they are not totally destroyed, surrender their normal autonomy of being and action to the body's higher organizing principle, its unitary substantial form. But, Father Clarke observes, they do not disappear completely and, on the dissolution of the complex whole, these lower elements re-emerge with the full autonomy of their proper action. St. Thomas himself had to admit that fact, and, under questioning about it, he allowed for a "virtual presence" of these elements in the complex whole.

This means that the unitary substantial form of the complex whole is not the formal act of a wholly undetermined potential principle, the "pure potency" which Aristotle and

Thomas called prime matter. What this form unifies is the "substantial potency" of lower organized systems plastic enough to surrender their autonomy of action to its higher organizing influence. At the bottom of the descending scale of systems may well be found the basic energy of our physical world organized by the ascending hierarchy of forms.[72]

Although, as Father Clarke concedes, some Thomists may have very serious reservations about his metaphysics of unitary substantial form and substantial potency, it does not seem, taken by itself, as radical a revision of Thomism as the one proposed in his metaphysics of essence and existence. He is far from being the first Thomist to admit the virtual presence of lower elements in substantial wholes, and support can be found in the text of St. Thomas himself for that admission. When, however, his revised metaphysics of matter and form is taken together with what he has already said about the partial surrender of a substantial form's autonomy to the higher form of the system in which the individual substance exists and acts, a number of provocative questions arise.

Substantial forms, existing in a system, it would appear, are organized by the form of the higher system, and they, in turn, organize the lower systems that exist "beneath them" in the complex whole. Is there, then, an ascending hierarchy of progressively higher systems, with some resemblance to the series of ascending systems progressively organized by a series of higher forms in Bernard Lonergan's metaphysics of emergent probability? If so, however, the series of unifications of lower systems by higher forms cannot proceed mechanically in a univocal way. For, in Father Clarke's metaphysics of the acting person, as in Father Lonergan's metaphysics of emergent probability, no subsisting human agent can be subordinated to the form of a higher physical or social system as an organic part is subordinated to the higher form of a living body.

The traditional categories of substance and accident, Norris Clarke tells us, can no longer handle the diverse set of relations between forms and systems. A new and more adequate category will be required to deal with their interrelation on the diverse levels of reality.[73] Nevertheless, both substance and accident are still required for Father Clarke's metaphysics of change. Yet, how is the category of substance to be defined more precisely, now that the relation of substantial form to subordinate lower systems has been "loosened up," and its relation to the forms of higher systems remains and must enter into its definition? There can be no doubt that, in Father Clarke's metaphysics, substance and substantial form still retain their pride of place. But the status of a formal principle of being, transcendentally related to prime matter, which defined the nature of substantial form for Thomists in the past, no longer defines its nature for Father Clarke. In his original philosophy of act and potency, as in the philosophy of Bernard Lonergan, the metaphysics of form and system has emerged as one of the most challenging developments in contemporary Thomism.

A "CREATIVE NEO-THOMIST"

Norris Clarke has described himself as a "creative Neo-Thomist."[74] And, as we have seen, in his philosophy of God, his metaphysics of relations, and his revised metaphysics of act and potency, there is ample evidence to support his claim. Unflagging intellectual curiosity and a remarkable openness of mind have made him an attentive listener to his colleagues in the philosophical community. Dialogue with them has enabled him to identify the weak spots in his inherited Thomism. A strong metaphysical mind has enabled him to make adjustments in it, required to meet the demands of contemporary experience, and to drop its outmoded elements without regret. For him, Thomism has not been a traditional "intellectual position"; it has been a living philosophy.

Open and creative as his Thomism has been, however, Norris Clarke is no eclectic. The metaphysics of participation and creation, grounded upon the interpersonal experience of the human agent, with which he began his intellectual career, has provided the backbone of his philosophy since then. He has held firmly to the original synthesis which he had worked out from his own experience of European Thomism, a personalist existential Thomism, enriched by the Transcendental Thomist tradition, but independent of it. In that original synthesis the act of existence, the dynamic ground of being's active self-presence, was the central perfection in which a community of limiting modes participated. Fidelity to its fundamental principles has been the source of the originality and power of his development of them through thirty-five years of teaching and writing. Norris Clarke has every right, then, to claim both titles, "creative" and "Neo-Thomist."

NOTES

1. For an excellent account of Descoqs' Suarezianism, see Helen James John, *The Thomist Spectrum* (New York: Fordham University Press, 1966), pp. 72–86. For Descoqs' epistemology, see George Van Riet, *L'Epistémologie thomiste* (Louvain: Editions de l'Institut Supérieur de Philosophie, 1946), pp. 377–87.

2. For André Marc's Thomism, see *Thomist Spectrum*, pp. 63–71. See also Gerald A. McCool, s.j., "Phenomenology and Dialectic: The Philosophy of André Marc, s.j.," *The Modern Schoolman*, 40 (1963), 321–45.

3. Maurice Blondel, *L'Action* (Paris: Alcan, 1893). Unobtainable for years, the 1893 edition of *L'Action* was reprinted in 1950 by Presses Universitaires de France. The University of Notre Dame Press brought out an English edition in 1984.

4. See *Thomist Spectrum*, pp. 32–41. See also Helen James John, "Emergence of the Act of Existing in Recent Thomism," *International Philosophical Quarterly*, 2 (1962), 600–25.

5. Etienne Gilson, *Being and Some Philosophers* (Toronto: Pontifical Institute of Mediaeval Studies, 1952), pp. 74–82.

6. *Being and Some Philosophers*, pp. 96–107.

7. *Being and Some Philosophers*, pp. 41–50.

8. *Being and Some Philosophers*, pp. 202–208.

9. Cornelio Fabro, *La Nozione metafisica di partecipazione secondo s. Tommaso d'Aquino* (Milan: Vita e Pensiero, 1939); a

second, revised edition was brought out by the Società Editrice Internazionale in 1959. For Fabro's metaphysics of participation in the act of existence, see *Thomist Spectrum*, pp. 87–107.

10. These were important themes in Gilson's interpretation of medieval philosophy. See Gilson's *The Spirit of Medieval Philosophy* (New York: Scribners, 1940), pp. 128–48.

11. *Spirit of Medieval Philosophy*, pp. 93–94. See also Gilson's *God and Philosophy* (New Haven: Yale University Press, 1941), pp. 57–73.

12. L.-B. Geiger, o.p., *La Participation dans la philosophie de s. Thomas d'Aquin* (Paris: Vrin, 1942). A second edition appeared in 1953. For Geiger's participation metaphysics, see *Thomist Spectrum*, pp. 108–22.

13. Louis De Raeymaeker, *La Philosophie de l'être* (Louvain: Editions de l'Institut Supérieur de Philosophie, 1947); trans. *The Philosophy of Being* (St. Louis: Herder, 1947). In this remarkable book the notion of participation served as the organizing principle for its treatment of finite being. For De Raeymaeker's participation metaphysics, see *Thomist Spectrum*, pp. 123–36.

14. Van Steenberghen's *Epistémologie* (Louvain: Editions de l'Institut Supérieur de Philosophie, 1945) appeared in several editions and was translated into a number of European languages; trans. *Epistemology* (New York: Wagner, 1949). His *Ontologie* (Louvain: Editions de l'Institut Supérieur de Philosophie, 1946) likewise appeared in a number of editions and was also translated into several European languages; trans. *Ontology* (New York: Wagner, 1970).

15. See Van Steenberghen's *Aristotle in the West* (Louvain: Nauwelaerts, 1955), pp. 147–62. See also his *The Philosophical Movement in the Thirteenth Century* (Edinburgh: Nelson, 1955), pp. 56–74; also *La Philosophie au XIIIᵉ siècle* (Louvain: Publications Universitaires, 1966), pp. 190–271.

16. Joseph de Finance, s.j., *Être et agir dans la philosophie de saint Thomas* (Paris: Beauchesne, 1945). For an account of de Finance and the Maréchalian recovery of *esse*, see *Thomist Spectrum*, pp. 151–58. For Father Clarke's praise of de Finance, see "The Limitation of Act by Potency," *The New Scholasticism*, 24 (1952), 167–94, esp. 168n2. See also "The Platonic Heritage of Thomism," *The Review of Metaphysics*, 8 (1954), 105–24, esp. 106n2.

17. Joseph de Finance, s.j., "Being and Subjectivity," *Cross Currents,* 6 (1956), 163–78.

18. Bernard J. F. Lonergan, s.j., *Insight: A Study of Human Understanding* (New York: Philosophical Library, 1957), p. xv.

19. For a defense of this position, written later in Norris Clarke's career, see "Interpersonal Dialogue: Key to Realism," in *Person and Community,* ed. Robert J. Roth, s.j. (New York: Fordham University Press, 1975), pp. 141–53.

20. "Recent European Trends in Metaphysics," *Proceedings of the Jesuit Philosophical Association,* 12 (1950), 48–73; "The Meaning of Participation in St. Thomas," *Proceedings of the Catholic Philosophical Association,* 26 (1952), 147–57. See also n. 16.

21. "What Is Really Real?," in *Progress in Philosophy,* ed. J. A. McWilliams (Milwaukee: Bruce, 1955), pp. 61–90.

22. "The Self in Eastern and Western Thought," *International Philosophical Quarterly,* 6 (1966), 101–109.

23. *The Philosophical Approach to God* (Winston-Salem: Wake Forest University, 1979), pp. 35–37.

24. "The Limitation of Act by Potency," 190–94.

25. See n. 21. Father Clarke returned to this controversial thesis in his "The Possibles Revisited," *The New Scholasticism,* 34 (1960), 79–102.

26. "Infinity in Plotinus: A Reply," *Gregorianum,* 50 (1959), 75–98.

27. Pierre Rousselot, s.j., *L'Intellectualisme de saint Thomas* (Paris: Beauchesne, 1936). The first edition of this celebrated work appeared in 1908. Rousselot was killed in action as a French soldier in 1915.

28. *L'Intellectualisme,* p. v.

29. See n. 19.

30. In Father Clarke's metaphysics, being manifests its active presence to the human subject through the immanent and transient action of intersubjective dialogue. Norris Clarke's metaphysics text, available up to now only in privately printed form, will be published by Fordham University Press.

31. "Analytical Philosophy and Knowledge of God," in *Christian Philosophy and Religious Renewal,* ed. George McLean, o.m.i. (Washington: The Catholic University of America Press, 1966), pp. 39–71, esp. pp. 48–49.

32. "Analytic Philosophy and Knowledge of God," pp. 49–50.

33. "The Natural Roots of Religious Experience," *Religious Studies*, 17 (1981), 511–23.

34. *Philosophical Approach to God*, pp. 35–37.

35. *Philosophical Approach to God*, p. 38. See also "Analytic Philosophy and Knowledge of God," pp. 65–66.

36. *Philosophical Approach to God*, pp. 17–28, 33–34.

37. *Philosophical Approach to God*, pp. 37–49.

38. "The Natural Roots of Religious Experience," 515–16.

39. "Analogy and the Meaningfulness of Language about God: A Reply to Kai Nielsen," *The Thomist*, 40 (1976), 61–95, esp. 87–88.

40. Hampus Lyttkens, *The Analogy between God and the World: An Investigation of its Background and Interpretation of Its Use by Thomas of Aquino* (Uppsala: Almqvist and Wiksell, 1952).

41. Bernard Montagnes, *L'Analogie de l'être d'après s. Thomas* (Louvain: Nauwelaerts, 1964).

42. George Klubertanz, *St. Thomas Aquinas on Analogy* (Chicago: Loyola University Press, 1960).

43. "Analogy and the Meaningfulness of Language about God," 85–88.

44. "Analytic Philosophy and Knowledge of God," pp. 61–62.

45. See nn. 31 and 39; also "Linguistic Analysis and Natural Theology," *Proceedings of the American Catholic Philosophical Association*, 34 (1960), 110–26.

46. See n. 33.

47. "Analogy and the Meaningfulness of Language about God," 81–83; *Philosophical Approach to God*, p. 48.

48. "Analogy and the Meaningfulness of Language about God," 73–74.

49. *Philosophical Approach to God*, pp. 51–52.

50. "Analogy and the Meaningfulness of Language about God," 83–84; *Philosophical Approach to God*, pp. 51–54.

51. *Philosophical Approach to God*, pp. 54–57.

52. *Philosophical Approach to God*, pp. 58–60.

53. *Philosophical Approach to God*, p. 54.

54. *Philosophical Approach to God*, p. 52.

55. "Analogy and the Meaningfulness of Language about God," 93–94.

56. "Analytic Philosophy and Knowledge of God," pp. 63–64.

57. "What is Most and Least Relevant in the Metaphysics of St. Thomas Today?," *International Philosophical Quarterly*, 14 (1974), 411–34, esp. 425–26.

58. "System: A New Category of Being," *Proceedings of the Jesuit Philosophical Association*, 24 (1962), 143–57.

59. Gerald A. McCool, s.j., ed., *A Rahner Reader* (New York: Seabury, 1975), pp. xxvi, 120–21.

60. "A New Look at the Immutability of God," in *God Knowable and Unknowable*, ed. Robert J. Roth, s.j. (New York: Fordham University Press, 1973), pp. 43–72.

61. See n. 21.

62. *Philosophical Approach to God*, p. 90.

63. *Philosophical Approach to God*, pp. 91–92.

64. *Philosophical Approach to God*, pp. 91–93.

65. *Philosophical Approach to God*, pp. 93–95.

66. Van Riet, *L'Epistémologie thomiste*, pp. 278–79.

67. "What is Most and Least Relevant . . . ," 425–30.

68. See also "What Cannot Be Said in St. Thomas' Essence–Existence Doctrine," *New Scholasticism*, 48 (1974), 19–39.

69. "What is Most and Least Relevant . . . ," 423–24.

70. It must be noted, however, that their objections were raised, not against Father Clarke's articles, but against the position of William Carlo, which Father Clarke favored with some reservations. See "What is Most and Least Relevant . . . ," 424n4.

71. "What is Most and Least Relevant . . . ," 426–27.

72. "What is Most and Least Relevant . . . ," 427–30.

73. "System: A New Category of Being."

74. *Philosophical Approach to God*, p. 92.

Fifty Years of Metaphysical Reflection: The Universe as Journey

W. NORRIS CLARKE, S.J.

Fordham University

LET ME BEGIN by expressing my deep appreciation for the invitation to speak on this especially gratifying occasion. First of all, I was invited to give the main philosophy lecture of the year, the Suarez Lecture, which is ordinarily reserved for a distinguished outside scholar. Secondly, I was offered the unusual and highly stimulating opportunity to look back on *my own career* of fifty years of philosophical—and especially metaphysical—reflection, to see if I can distill the main themes and abiding attitudes that have marked my thinking throughout all these years. I assure you, it is quite an experience to take one's own thought as a topic to reflect on objectively, and not just the thought of someone else or some problem in philosophy, which is the ordinary occupation of most of us philosophers. I must say that I have found the process of responding to this invitation—of trying to discern in the history of my own thought a meaningful story—a task at once fascinating, challenging, illuminating, and—a bit surprisingly—joyful. Perhaps you too will find it of some interest to share this experience with me.

What I intend to do is not to give you a history of my own philosophical development. That might be of some interest, too, but more of an historical kind, and more for friends and those who have known me fairly well. I would like rather to make a positive philosophical statement in its own right, focusing on the great central themes that have remained more or less constant throughout my roughly fifty years of reflection on metaphysical topics, and indicating why I consider them important and central. I hope this might stimulate each one of you who heard or reads this to reflect on what—if any—have been the central abiding themes in your own intellectual history.

IS THERE A NATURAL PREDISPOSITION TO METAPHYSICS?

Before plunging directly into the six major themes that have dominated my metaphysical history, I would like to touch briefly on the interesting psychological question of whether there is, as some claim, a personal psychological predisposition toward metaphysical thinking, something like a *metaphysical bent of mind*. I think everyone can profit from some basic exposure to metaphysical problems—that is why we have this subject as one of our core courses at Fordham College—but it is also clear to me that not everyone has the aptitude or the inner attraction to become a self-propelling, self-motivated metaphysician in the fuller sense. There *is*, then, I believe, a certain natural aptitude, affinity, or bent of mind that can be called metaphysical. What are its benchmarks? Looking back over my own history I can discern clearly enough the following—and my own informal investigation leads me to believe that many other metaphysicians can testify to something similar.

I. *A passion for unity*, for seeing how the universe and all things in it *fit together as a whole,* a meaningful whole, a longing for integration of thought and life based on the integration of reality itself. One of the characteristic ways this manifested itself in my life was through the love of high places. On the surface, indeed, all through my youth up to the end of high school I appeared to be a normally adjusted boy who enjoyed playing sports with the neighborhood kids or in school. But in addition I always had to get away periodically by myself to think, always alone, and, if possible, in the highest place around. In my grammar-school days these were the trees in Riverside Park (in Manhattan, before the West Side Highway was built), near which I grew up. I soon knew all the highest and most climbable ones, and spent hours in their tops meditating in my own simple untutored way on "things." For some inexplicable reason it was against the law to climb trees in the park, but when the local cop on the park beat would spot me, come under the tree, and order me down, I soon learned that I could simply challenge him to come up and get me—which I knew was beyond his corpulent capabilities—and since they had no walkie-talkies in those days to call for help, he would soon tire of his vigil and walk away. My older brother—who was very intelligent but not given at all to metaphysical thinking—once asked me: "What are you thinking about up there?" "Things," I answered. "What things?," he persisted. "Well, sort of everything," I replied. "But how can you think about things you don't know anything about?" "I don't know," I answered uncomfortably; "you just sort of listen." He sadly gave up further probing into my intellectual life from that time on.

As I grew older in high school I discovered much higher places, like the cliffs of the Palisades across the Hudson River, and the great towers of the George Washington Bridge, up which I climbed some 300 feet from the river bed below. From here one could get a magnificent wide vista. Later on when I became a Jesuit I was able to graduate to real mountains, taking the occasion whenever I could. I will never forget when I was a young Jesuit philosophy student studying in France and took the summer off to learn German in the Jesuit Novitiate of Feldkirch in Austria. A young Swiss priest vacationing there offered to take a Spaniard and me on a climb to the top of the Schesaplana, a lovely 10,000-foot Alp on the border between Switzerland and Austria, across whose rugged folds many refugees escaped during the war. We walked all afternoon, slowly and methodically, till at nine o'clock at

night, after making our way in pitch dark across a two-foot
ledge along the face of the mountain with a 2,000-foot sheer
drop on one side, we (nourished by brandy and chocolate)
finally pulled into a climbers' bunkhouse at 9,500 feet, slept
there overnight, and next morning walked across a small gla-
cier and up the last 500 feet to the summit just as the sun rose
over the vast expanse of surrounding snow-capped Alps. The
spectacle was of such grandeur, sublimity, and upward-soaring
beauty that it seemed to purge my spirit of attachment to anything base, mean, ignoble, or beneath the full nobility and
unlimited horizons to which the human spirit, I felt, was
called. This experience left an indelible mark on my whole
intellectual and also personal life.

Later on, back home, mountains, either climbed or viewed,
have again punctuated my career as a philosopher: for example, my beloved Mt. Mansfield in Stowe, Vermont, to whose
summit I have been drawn by some quasi-mystical attraction a
half-dozen times or more; or the 70-mile spectacular drive over
the 10,000-foot-high Beartooth Pass into Yellowstone Park,
and the dream-like Grand Teton mountains reflected in Jenny
Lake. Finally, late in my career I was able to fulfill my childhood dream—which I had always thought would be only a
dream—of seeing "the great mountains," the Himalayas. On a
memorable trip to India with college professors (paid for by
the State Department in the more halcyon days of Democratic
spending), we were able to catch in perfect weather what has
long been celebrated as one of the greatest views on this earth:
the sun rising over the Himalayas from the vantage point of
Tiger Hill (11,000 feet, near Darjeeling), touching the great
peaks one by one first with red, then pink, then gold, then
white, till finally Mt. Everest itself lit up 100 miles away. All
our words were stilled, even for college professors. Again, on
another trip to India, when I slipped off to Nepal between
two philosophical conferences, I made sure to take in what is
certainly one of the most beautiful airplane flights in the
world, the famous "Mt. Everest Flight" in a tiny Royal Nepal-
ese airplane right along the great mountains, including Mt.

Everest (the best-spent $30 in my life). The beauty became so overwhelming at one point that I had to close my eyes, lest I explode from within.

But what precisely is the connection between mountains and metaphysics? For me at least—and I have found a similar experience in other metaphysicians—to look out over the countryside from a high place enables one to see *how it all fits together*, making a single overall pattern. From down below, streams, valleys, hills, etc. all seem to be doing their own thing somewhat separately, without their interconnections' being that visible. From higher up, it becomes clear how they all weave together to form a whole. The higher viewpoint yields the unity. This visual physical experience seems to be a kind of symbol, a foretaste, an acting-out on the physical level, of the inner spiritual synoptic vision of how all things in the universe somehow fit together to make an integrated meaningful whole. It is a kind of physical practice for doing metaphysics.

This love of high places and its significance for the metaphysical bent of mind is not at all peculiar to me, I have found. Many metaphysicians have a similar affinity. I once read an informal study on the connections between metaphysicians and mountains; it seems that mountains have played a key role in the life and thought of a large number of metaphysicians. St. Thomas, for example, was brought at the age of six to be educated at the famous Benedictine abbey of Monte Cassino, perched way on the top of a large mountain, looking out over a wide vista of towns, streams, mountains, and valleys. Closer to home, when I asked my colleague Dr. Elizabeth Kraus, certainly a high-flying metaphysician in her own right, if she was interested in mountains or saw any connection with metaphysics, she answered as though surprised, "But of course; didn't you know I was a mountain climber and loved mountains? Of course there is a connection."

So I think the evidence is good for a natural affinity between metaphysicians and high places, preferably mountains. All philosophers may not have the same preference. Some may prefer streams, lakes, the ocean, the plains, possibly even the swamps. The ideal setting, it occurs to me, for working out a Derrida-type Deconstructionist theory would seem to me to be the misty half-gloom and shifting quicksand of an Everglades swamp. But we will venture no further on this uncertain ground . . .

II. The second predisposition toward a metaphysical bent of mind has been in my case—and similarly for many other metaphysicians—a sense of some kind of *overall hidden harmony of the universe*, which could be picked up and possibly spelled out if one listened carefully enough. As a teenager, sitting on my lofty perch on the Palisade cliffs over the Hudson, I felt there was something great going on *under the surface* of things, some kind of hidden music, some harmony of all things that I could not quite hear but somehow knew was there and longed to lay hold of in my consciousness. The mountains on the surface manifested the unity in a visual image; what was hidden under the surface manifested itself in an auditory image.

This notion of the hidden harmony within all things, of the universe itself as an integral, patterned—though not alalways obvious—harmony, is one of the oldest and richest of all philosophical and humanistic ideas. It burst forth very early in Greek philosophy in the West with the genial Pythagorean vision of a universe held together in unity by harmony both ontologically and ethically; it emerged from other sources with equal seminal power in ancient Chinese and other Oriental thought-systems. This great, primordial, archetypal image–feeling–idea has always had a very powerful attraction for me. To give some articulate, conceptual expression to this deep-lying intuitive awareness and trust in the hidden harmony of the Whole has always been one of the powerful motivating forces behind my own natural attraction for doing metaphysics. And even though Nietzsche is by no means one of my favorite philosophers, I recently discovered to my surprise that he had put this very point beautifully in the following magnificently pithy sentence: "The philosopher seeks to hear the echoes of the World Symphony and reproject it into concepts." This is exactly what the metaphysician, pre-eminently among philosophers, is trying to do, with his elaborately constructed conceptual systems. This helps to explain why, even though someone has shown flaws in the conceptual working-out of a metaphysician's system, this does not discourage him for long. He goes back again to listen to the harmony, which for him is beyond refutation, to see if he can express it more adequately.

So much for the interesting question of a natural predisposition for metaphysical thinking, which I think has solid grounds not only in my own experience but in that of many other metaphysicians, such as Whitehead in our own day, in whom it is most strikingly manifested by his choice of harmony as a leitmotif of his entire thought. Now let us plunge more directly into my own metaphysical vision, developed over the last fifty years of explicit philosophizing.

BRIEF OVERVIEW OF MY METAPHYSICAL DEVELOPMENT

First, just a quick note on what I understand "metaphysics" to mean, since the meaning has shifted considerably for many in contemporary philosophy. For many today, especially in analytic circles, the term "metaphysics" does not stand for any unified systematic branch of philosophical knowledge, but is taken merely as a grabbag for all those problems concerning the way things are (thus excluding how our minds work—espistemology—and how we should act—ethics), which cannot be solved by observation or scientific investigation: e.g., the body–mind problem, the existence of God, free will, idealism–realism, etc. I take metaphysics in the older classical sense, which it has had since Aristotle. Philosophy as such, in general, I take to be the systematic effort to illuminate our experience in depth and set it in a vision of the whole. More informally, it is a person taking reflective possession of him- or herself and his or her place in the universe as a whole.

Metaphysics is that part of philosophy which attends explicitly to the vision of the whole, which tries to lay out the great general laws and principles governing all beings and rendering them intelligible, including what it means to be real at all. Thus I stand squarely in the great tradition of *systematic* metaphysics as the fundamental ground of all philosophy, whose aim is precisely to spell out systematically the vision of reality as a meaningful whole (or, of course, the lack of such meaning, for some, like Sartre).

Let me indicate very briefly now the main phases I went through in my own metaphysical development. My initiation into metaphysical thinking took place in the French Jesuit house of philosophical studies on the island of Jersey in the English Channel, where I was introduced to the creative systematic Thomism of André Marc, a powerful and brilliant metaphysical mind.[1] He had made his own original synthesis of the new Transcendental Thomism movement stemming from Maréchal (stressing the radical dynamism of the mind toward all of being and its Infinite Source) and the similar doctrine of Maurice Blondel applied to the dynamism of the will, as an introduction and underpinning to the traditional structure of Thomistic metaphysics. The latter included the real distinction of essence and existence in all creatures, analogy, act and potency, matter and form, substance and accident, efficient and final causality, and the primacy of personal being. My two greatest and most deeply formative metaphysical experiences were reading on my own the four volumes then extant of Joseph Maréchal's great *summa* of Transcendental Thomism, *Le Point de départ de la métaphysique* (relating the whole of Western philosophical history to the central theses in Thomism, reinterpreted in the light of the radical dynamism of the mind toward the Infinite), and Maurice Blondel's powerful and seminal work, *L'Action* (1893). Since Blondel was under a cloud with the ecclesiastical guardians of orthodoxy at the time, his book, quickly out of print, was banned for us, and the only way to read it was to get into an inner circle of initiates who passed a contraband typed copy from one to the other to be read at night. Under the impact of these two great works and Marc's teaching, my metaphysical mind expanded rapidly like a thirsty flower, and by the end of my three years there (at the ripe age of 24), the main pieces of my philosophical vision suddenly seemed to fall into place, and I felt I was now a metaphysician in my own right, with my own basic metaphysical vision firmly in place, though with many gaps still to be filled in. I cannot be too grateful for this rich and creative early Thomistic formation that gave me my "sea legs" as a philosopher.

Graduate school in Louvain eight years later added four new distinctive contributions to this foundation: (1) I came to appreciate more explicitly, in its full originality, power, and historical grounding, the existential turn of St. Thomas in setting the act of existence at the center of his whole philosophical system. This I gained through the reading of Gilson and de Finance,[2] masters of this crucial new turn in the interpretation of St. Thomas that surfaced only from 1939 on. (2) I also discovered for the first time the Neoplatonic dimension of St. Thomas' participation doctrine—revealing his original synthesis of both Aristotle and Neoplatonism—another crucial new turn in Thomistic interpretation that was just surfacing at the same time through the work of Geiger, Fabro, and de Finance (never really accepted, however, by the Gilson school).[3] (3) I came to realize the absolutely central role of action not only for binding together all things into a universe but also for grounding the link of our minds with reality. (4) I soaked myself deeply for a while in the currently exploding Existentialist movement, and especially in the French Existential Personalists (Marcel, Mounier, Nédoncelle) and Martin Buber, with a powerful awakening to the central role not only of the person in general but especially of the intersubjective dimension of the person. I have ever since placed the "We are . . . in dialogue" as the basic anti-Cartesian starting-point of my whole epistemology and metaphysics. Later on in my teaching career came the discovery and dialogue with both process philosophy and Oriental thought.

We are now ready to tackle directly the main themes that have dominated my metaphysical reflection over the last 50 years, themes that are central in my philosophical vision of the universe. These themes I have boiled down to six. There is no magic number involved in this; it is merely that I find I cannot simplify further, though it would certainly be easy to expand to many more. (1) The first is an underlying presupposition in the metaphysician himself for engaging in the metaphysical enterprise at all: this is the *unrestricted dynamism of the inquiring mind* to understand all of being. The next five are what might be called the basic pillars of reality itself, central aspects without which it cannot be understood, to my mind, without gross distortion or crippling omission. They are: (2) *existence* conceived as the dynamic act of presence that binds together all real things; (3) the *participation structure* of the universe, which allows there to be many different beings all sharing in common some common attribute; (4) *action*, which is the self-manifestation of each thing's inner being and makes its presence felt to other beings in the universe, that which makes this to be an interconnected and communicating universe; (5) *the good*, which is the goal and purpose of the universe and of each thing in it, the universal magnet that lures each being to overflow into action; and (6) *the person*, or the universe as radically personalized, from and for persons as the supreme value in the universe. These five central themes will then be woven together into a guiding image of the universe as a whole in action, which will be that of a journey, *the journey of all being from the One and back to the One.*

1. *The Unrestricted Dynamism of the Mind toward Being*
By this I mean the deep natural drive of the human mind to

lay hold of intellectually and understand as far as possible the entire order of being, all there is to know about all there is. This drive knows no limits short of the total understanding of all being, both in depth and in breadth. We can discover this unrestricted drive within ourselves if we reflect carefully on the life of our minds. When we come to know something new, we first explore it, savor it, enjoy our discovery; but as soon as we reach the limits of the thing in question, discover that it has limits, the mind naturally rebounds beyond to something more. And so on and on until we reach the totality of all being. The natural correlative of the human mind is being itself in all its fullness; the human mind, as the medieval Scholastics put it so succinctly, is *capax entis*, or *potens omnia fieri* (quoting Aristotle).[4] The mind's theme song, we might say, is: "Don't fence me in!" A similar natural drive exists in the complementary faculty of the human spirit, the will, which has an unrestricted desire to possess the fullness of all being as good.

This seminal idea of the unrestricted dynamism of the human spirit toward the fullness of being was first introduced to me by the reading of Maréchal and Blondel and the synthesis of André Marc in my first philosophical training on the island of Jersey. And I quickly came to realize that it was the underlying dynamo, the mainspring energizing the whole project of metaphysical inquiry, in fact the entire life of inquiry of the human mind in any field—though not realized in its unlimited scope outside of metaphysics. I have made it the launching-pad of my own metaphysical system ever since.[5]

Matching this natural drive of the mind toward being, if it is not to be radically frustrated, is the complementary aptitude or openness of all being to be known, otherwise known as the intrinsic intelligibility of being, all being. This does not mean that I or any other human or finite mind will actually succeed in fully understanding all being, or any part of it, at least in this life. But it does mean that all being is of itself *open*, in principle, to being known; it is in principle, at least, intel-lig*ible*; it is not of itself radically closed to intelligence, contrary to it, absurd. Mind is for being, and reciprocally being is for mind. Just how this possession of being is to be achieved in any particular case, whether by rational inquiry, intuitive insight, metaphysical experience, or whatever, cannot be decided ahead of time. This principle of the radical intelligibility of being can be made to open out at once into what has been traditionally known as the Principle of Sufficient Reason: i.e., every being must have a sufficient reason, something that renders intelligible why it *is* and *is such*, either within itself or in some other (its adequate cause). Such a principle is the dynamo behind all metaphysical inquiry, behind every "Why?" question. It cannot, of course, be logically proved before we start inquiring. But it is a kind of lived existential necessity for any serious exercise of the mind, as Einstein and so many other great scientists have admitted; the very dynamic pull of our minds draws us naturally to accept it and live by it, implicitly or explicitly, by a certain "natural faith." To deny it explicitly is to cut the nerve of any intellectual inquiry, since every inquiry presupposes, at least implicitly, that there is something there to be understood; it is to fall into a lived—not a logical—contradiction if we then continue to use our minds to solve problems. To function at all as rational beings in a real universe we did not make, our first move must be at least implicitly to accept with humility and gratitude the intellectual nature that has been given to us, with its built-in natural correlation with the domain of being as in principle open to the light of mind, intelligible in itself.

This absolutely fundamental mutual correlation of mind and being, mind for being and being for mind, has been beautifully termed by Maritain a "nuptial relation," a natural marriage made in heaven, so to speak, where each partner completes the other. But notice the appropriate roles in this marriage: the human mind is analogously like the female, the mother; reality is like the father. To know truly a reality that it has not itself made, the mind must make itself open to receive this reality, to be actively informed by it. The mind, fecundated, informed, by reality, then actively responds, pours its own spiritual life into what it receives, gestates, then gives birth to the mental "word" or concept, which in turn flows over into the verbal word expressed to others. Notice the deep insight encapsulated in this ancient term "concept": It is not by accident that this mental word has been traditionally called a "concept": for to know is for the mind to conceive and give birth to an inner mental word expressing the real that has informed it, and bearing the features of both parents—reality and the mind. Thus *theoretical* intelligence (knowing the world as it already is) is more like a *she*; *practical* intelligence, on the other hand, as ordered toward guiding some act of making or doing on the part of the knower, is more like a *he*, since it actively changes or re-creates the world through creative initiative and action.

It is because of my belief in this "nuptial relationship" between the mind and reality that I feel such antipathy toward the epistemology of Immanuel Kant. For despite the many partial insights of Kant, Kantian epistemology seems to me at root what can be called an *anti-feminist* epistemology. Rather than allowing reality to reveal itself to the human mind by actively informing it, the Kantian mind is more like an aggressive all-male activist, actively imposing its own pre-fabricated *a priori* forms on the disordered raw material of the sense manifold coming into it. Rather than a receptive, nurturing mother, it is more like an extroverted male construction worker remaking the world according to his own wishes and plans. At least in the realm of epistemology, therefore, it seems to me that the feminine model of the mind as mother enshrines a much deeper and more accurate insight into the fundamental relationship between the mind and reality than the Kantian masculine model.

2. *Existence as the Act of Presence*
By this I mean the rediscovery, or new highlighting, of the "act of existence"—the *esse* or "to be" of things, as St. Thomas insists on putting it—as the central vantage-point of the entire

Thomistic philosophical vision of the universe—a rediscovery now almost universally accepted by Thomists since the combined work of Gilson, Maritain (to a somewhat lesser extent), de Finance, Marc, Geiger, Fabro, De Raeymaeker, etc., and widely publicized in this country by disciples of the Gilson–Toronto school and those of Louvain Existential Thomism like myself.[6] This basic Thomistic insight shifts the whole center of gravity from form and essence, which had been the central focus of attention of all the great metaphysicians from Plato on, including Aristotle, to existence itself, seen as the radical underlying act of presence in each real being by which all real beings are real—i.e., actually present in the universe and actively present to all other real beings. It is the most fundamental common attribute that all real things share, deeper even than form or essence, that which makes them stand out sharply and distinctly from the surrounding darkness and emptiness of non-being and become a member of this most ultimate of all communities, the community of all real existents.

Notice that this principle of existence is not a form or structure in things, a "what," but rather an inner dynamic *act* of presence that makes all forms or structures actually present as diverse modes of the radical "energy" of existence (St. Thomas calls it by the powerful term, later picked up by Paul Tillich, *virtus essendi*, "the power of being"). This act of presence naturally flows over to express itself in action according to the being's essence, thus making every being, because of its inner act of existence, an *active presence* to the community of other existents in the universe. This means that every real being, in virtue of its in-dwelling act of existence, has the power to express itself, relate itself to the rest of the universe, communicate its own existential energy to other beings. In a word, "to be" means not only to be actually present, but to be a *presence-with-power*, a *power-filled presence* in the world. Thus active power is inseparable from existence; it is impossible to be at all without some proportionate power. It is precisely this notion of existence as active, power-filled presence that renders *degrees of being* possible—a notion that so many philosophers, especially analytic, find baffling, since for them "to be" signifies nothing more than the bare, minimum brute fact of existence.

The implications of this metaphysics of existence as act also provide the key to unlock the whole nature of Divine Being for St. Thomas. God is now seen as the pure subsistent Act of Existence, unlimited by any finite form or essence, and by that very fact becomes the supreme concentration of existential energy in the universe that both makes present and energizes all other beings in the universe.

To bring into explicit focus, however, this deep-lying act of existence at the core of every being, as the ultimate bond of union between all real things, does not come easily to a common-sense vision of the world, more concerned with *what* things are and *how* they act than *that* they are. There is required a kind of "metaphysical conversion to existence" (as some Thomists have aptly put it), a reflective "listening" to beings under their aspect of actual presence as standing out of nothingness, an awakening of the sense of wonder at the marvel that anything is actually present at all, or, as Heidegger put it so well, "the wonder of all wonders, that anything exists at all, rather than nothing."[7] Is not the poet Shelley thinking of the same thing when he warns us that "The mist of familiarity obscures from us the wonder of our being"?[8] Long before I ever read Heidegger, I remember being deeply moved by the remark of a French metaphysician, Marcel de Corte, writing on the spirit of Gabriel Marcel's philosophy: "If from his first step, from his first glance at the least of beings, the metaphysician does not feel himself confusedly on the edge of a sacred abyss, then let him close his eyes; he is not worthy of this humble thing that he contemplates."[9]

To bring about this metaphysical conversion to existence requires that the mind shift its reflective awareness from the initial common-sense understanding of existence as merely the *fact* of existence (the *truth* that something is there outside the mind), beyond which even many philosophers never seem to get, to the recognition of that which *grounds* this fact *inside* the thing itself, the being's own *inner act* of existence. Many philosophers, including metaphysicians—this is especially noticeable among analytic philosophers—seem never quite to have made this passage. This awakening can theoretically be done on one's own; but in practice some kind of guide is usually needed to point the way, to show us where and how to look at things, until existence itself as act suddenly lights up and comes alive in our consciousness.[10] St. Thomas himself, in fact, in one of his profoundly illuminating passing remarks while commenting on the Pseudo-Dionysius, likens the actual existence of a thing to "a kind of light," by which it shines forth to other things.[11] Thus all finite beings, he tells us, because they have an act of existence, are "lit up, shining" (*lucentia*), but because they are not the source of their own existence they are not "the light itself" (*ipsa lux*). Only God is that. This philosophical awakening to the primacy of the act of existence as the deepest level in every being and the ultimate bond of unity between all things, with all its systematic implications for God, the theory of knowledge, etc., is the great central pillar of St. Thomas' and of my own metaphysical vision of the universe.[12]

3. *Participation*

By participation I mean the basic ontological structure of sharing in the universe, by which many beings share diversely in some one common positive property or "perfection" (as the medievals called it), thus making a unified group or community of some kind. Such a participation structure is a One in many. The systematic conceptualization of it is one of the great legacies of the Platonic and especially the Neoplatonic tradition, inspired by Plotinus and Proclus, its masters. Put very briefly, it involves the inner composition in any participating being of two complementary components or co-principles: one representing the common unifying perfection shared by all—say, existence, life, intelligence, human nature, etc.— and the other representing the limiting receiving subject which receives this common perfection in a particularized limited way according to its own capacity of reception. All the members of the group sharing the same participation structure are then further unified by sharing the same one transcendent ultimate source from which this common shared perfection flows. Thus the immanent One *in* many is also a many *from* a transcendent One. This source possesses the perfection it has ultimately imparted to the others, not in a limited imperfect way, but rather in its pure unlimited fullness, so that it is more proper to say that it *is* the perfection in question, rather than that it *has* it. St. Thomas took over this whole systematic participation structure from Neoplatonism in order to complete and enrich the Aristotelian theory of change. The latter had deliberately rejected all participation of a lower in a higher world because of its initial association with the Platonic separated world of subsistent pure ideas as the really real—a doctrine anathema to Aristotle, for reasons not necessary to explain here. But Thomas' genius was to apply this old Platonic doctrine, originally focused on participation in idea or form, to his own new concept of the act or energy of existence as the ultimate ground and bond of unity of all things.[13]

Thus the whole universe appears as a vast participation system, a *One in many* which is also a *many from One*. It appears as an immense diversity of distinct real beings, each with its own inner existential energy, so to speak, which also binds it by a natural similitude and affinity to all other real beings, but which in each case is limited, diversified, and molded by its own particular limiting essence, or determinate mode-of-being. This is the famous Thomistic doctrine of the real distinction and composition of essence and existence in all finite beings, grounded ultimately in one pure unlimited subsistent Act of Existence as the ultimate Source of all being. This is the very center of the whole Thomistic vision of the universe, both philosophically and theologically—and, we might add, mystically. This is for St. Thomas—and for me, too—what Bergson described so beautifully as that single simple centerpoint of every great philosopher's thought, which he tried over and over to express in different ways all his life, and never quite succeeded:

> But as we seek to penetrate more fully the philosopher's thought instead of circling around its exterior, his doctrine is transformed for us. In the first place its complication diminishes. Then the various parts fit into one another. Finally the whole is brought together into a single point, which we feel could be ever more closely approached even though there is no hope of reaching it completely. In this point is something simple, infinitely simple, so extraordinarily simple that the philosopher has never succeeded in saying it. And this is why he went on talking all his life.[14]

Hence its full significance, beauty, and power are not yet grasped as long as it is seen merely as a dry technical problem and solution to a conceptual puzzle of the One and the many. To come alive in the mind—and, I might add, the imagination, which I believe has a hidden, not always recognized, but very important role in metaphysics—it must be seen as a synoptic vision of the universe, in which all beings, from the lowest to the highest, come together to form a single great community, where each holds the common identification card of the act of existence, or active presence, plus its own individual signature as a distinct member of this ultimate club of real being, where everything has secret affinities with everything else from highest to lowest, where nothing real can ever be objectively alienated in any ultimate way. In a word, "To be is to be together," or, as a contemporary artist put it to me, "To be is the act of belonging."[15] Togetherness and community are woven into the very stuff of all being, as being.

A significant consequence, to me, in view of the work of Teilhard de Chardin, is that there is no radical split even between matter and spirit, because both are in the last analysis only different degrees or modalities of the common energy, or force-filled presence, of existence itself. For if the act of existence is the radical underlying ground and bond of all being, and each real being is, to the degree that it exists, in some way an image, however imperfect, of the ultimate Pure

66

Act of Existence, then every single being, no matter how lowly in the material domain or lofty in the spiritual, must somehow have deep hidden similitudes and affinities with every other. Here is the underlying metaphysical grounding of metaphor in poetry, literature, and indeed all the arts. For if psyche mirrors nature and nature mirrors psyche, each in its own way, then comparison with either can illuminate the other. Thus "a smiling field" illuminates nature by psyche, whereas "a stormy face" illuminates psyche by nature. This mutual mirroring of psyche and nature seems to me the very heart of metaphor.[16]

A final brief word on the ascent to the Source of all being in this participation metaphysics, that is, to God understood metaphysically.[17] When we look more deeply into the universe as a single great participation system, the question naturally arises, from the application of the natural drive of the mind toward total understanding of all being, "What is the ultimate ontological grounding or sufficient reason for this radical immanent unity running through the entire universe of real beings?" In one of his central metaphysical paths of ascent of the mind to God from the finite world of our experience, St. Thomas lays down the general premiss, drawn directly from Neoplatonism, that in any system where many beings share some real common property, the objective similarity of all cannot be explained *because* they are diverse and many. Similarity is a form of unity, and it cannot be ultimately *because* they are *diverse and many* that they are *similar*, and thus one, in some way. This unity of similarity must ultimately be grounded in some real *One* that contains the common perfection in question in full unlimited plenitude as a Source from which it flows actively (i.e., by efficient causality, in Aristotelian terms) to all the participants. Applying this general premiss now to the underlying common perfection of existence in all things, the drive of minds toward intelligibility leads us to posit, by a compelling intellectual exigency or insight, one supreme Ultimate Source of all existence, which possesses the fullness of existential energy in a single subsistent, pure Act of Existence, or, if you wish, pure "I am" (the most appropriate of all names for God, St. Thomas says).

This ascent to God through participation, from the many to the One in the order of existence, and the similar alternate ascent moving explicitly from the finite to the Infinite, are unfortunately not clearly and effectively put forward in St. Thomas' famous Five Ways, which I confess to finding much too Aristotelian, incomplete, and unsatisfactory for modern man, although the argument from degrees of being (the Fourth) can be much more cogently formulated, as St. Thomas has done elsewhere, and the Fifth argument from order in the world can easily be completed by St. Thomas' developments elsewhere. From this basic notion of God as pure infinite Act of Existence and thus Source of all being follows the entire Thomistic philosophy of God, His attributes, and His relation to the world, although I do think more stress on the personal being of God is needed to correct what I feel is the too heavy and one-sided development of the immutability aspect of God's perfection in St. Thomas' own texts.

In view of this participation doctrine of the immanent and transcendent unity of the universe as deriving from one infinite Source that is pure Act of Existence, all real things now not only become partial mirrorings or images of each other but more centrally are also imperfect images of the one Source. The whole universe thus becomes a single great hierarchically ordered community or "family" with the same Father. Thus we find a rich and creative synthesis between the Biblical image doctrine of all creation, especially man, and the more technical metaphysical doctrine of participation. The Book of Creation and the Book of Revelation echo each other. A richly humanistic creation spirituality naturally flows out of this.

4. Action

The next central pillar of reality and our explanation of it is action, the activity by which the various centers of existential energy in the universe pour over into self-expression and self-communication with each other. It was not till graduate school in Louvain, principally through the reading of Joseph de Finance's great book, *Être et agir*, and through continuously deepening metaphysical reflection thereafter, that I slowly came to realize the absolutely central role of action for an integrated metaphysical vision of the universe.[18] Without action all we would have would be a collection of isolated beings, each a center of existential energy similar to all others, but totally bound up within itself, with no connection or communication with others, and hence no way of knowing them. Every being would be plunged in total silence and darkness as far as the rest of the universe is concerned, a total "black hole," so to speak, except that it would not even exert any gravitational pull on the rest, as black holes do in our world. It is action alone that enables beings to come out of their isolation, connect with each other, influence each other, and communicate to each other. It is action that actually shows forth the hidden inner unity of similitude between things coming from their constitution as participants in existence. It is action that truly allows there to be a *universe*, that is, a turning of all toward oneness, togetherness.

Let us unfold this a bit. What is the connection of action with being for St. Thomas, and for me, since this has now become so inseparably a part of my own thought and vision of the universe? Action, as self-communicative, self-expressive activity, flows directly out of the very act of existence that is the inner core of all real beings. Linking his own original doctrine of existence as the act of presence with the ancient Platonic and Neoplatonic tradition of the Good as naturally self-diffusive, self-communicating, St. Thomas sees every real being, because of its inner energy of existential act, as possessed of a natural dynamism to pour over into self-expressive action, which communicates its own perfection as far as it can to others, in turn receiving from them—if it is finite—what they have to give: *agere sequitur esse* (action follows upon being), as the ancient adage goes. In the Neoplatonic tradition the Good itself was above and beyond being, which was identified with the order of limited essences; St. Thomas fuses the two together more integrally, so that goodness is no longer something other than or higher than being. Rather, existential being itself, of its very nature, is good, and thus has this self-diffusive character to it, from the highest to the lowest. Thus God for St. Thomas is at once supreme Act of Existence and by that very fact supreme Goodness also. Over and over again in different contexts he comes back to this favorite theme of the natural self-communication and self-expression of being through action. For example:

> It is in the nature of every actuality to communicate itself insofar as it is possible. Hence every agent acts according as it exists in act.[19]
>
> From the very fact that something exists in act, it is active.[20]
>
> Communication follows upon the very nature of actuality.[21]
>
> To bring forth an actuality is, of itself, proper to a being in act; for every agent acts according as it is in act. Therefore every being in act is by its nature apt to bring forth something actual. . . . Actual existence is the source of all action.[22]
>
> To each thing pertains its own proper operation according as it possesses the act of existence, so that each and every thing operates insofar as it is a being.[23]
>
> Each and every thing shows forth that it exists for the sake of its operation; indeed operation (activity) is the ultimate perfection of each thing.[24]
>
> The nature of each and every thing is shown forth by its operation.[25]
>
> The operation of a thing manifests both its substance (essence) and its existence.[26]
>
> The substantial forms of things, which are unknown to us as they are in themselves, shine forth to us [innotescunt] through their accidental properties (i.e., operations, etc.).[27]

This fusion of being itself with self-diffusive, self-communicating goodness is what brings all real beings together into one great intercommunicating network of giving and receiving, acting on and being acted on, which makes the realm of real being precisely a *Universe* of things *turned toward each other* to make a dynamically unified system. Without action beings would be cut off from each other, buried in the loneliness of their own isolation, would make no difference to each other. To be is *to make a difference* to others. That is why, too, action is the basic necessary and sufficient criterion for distinguishing between truly real beings and merely mental beings, ideas, mental constructions, possibilities, etc. Ideas cannot act of themselves; real beings can— they are by nature agents. That is the single most important critique of the entire Platonic tradition, to my mind: since the Platonic ideas cannot act, they cannot, important as they are, be the "really real." They can, however, become ingredient in the real by becoming active forms, the intelligible structure of action.

The depth, fecundity, and absolutely central role of action both for being and for our knowledge of it, for metaphysics and epistemology, cannot be overestimated, to my mind, especially in view of its being so underplayed and underexploited in so much modern Western philosophical thought since Descartes, in particular in the theory of knowledge. The essential core of all Thomistic epistemology (at least my version of it, which I think is solidly grounded in the texts) can be summed up in one sentence: All knowledge of the real is an interpretation of action—period! There is simply no way a real being can make itself known except through its self-expression, its self-revelation, through its characteristic actions. I know myself as real because I am aware of *myself acting* (thinking, desiring, willing, creating, etc.); I know other things than myself by knowing them as *acting on me* in such and such a way, plus all the further implications needed to understand this action as fully intelligible. Although we cannot conceptually identify being and self-expressive action, still if a being did not act at all, it would remain in total isolation and darkness as far as the rest of the world is concerned: the ultimate "black hole," so to speak, giving no sign of its presence at all. Since it would make no difference to anything else in the universe, it might just as well not be at all. There would be no way at all of knowing that it was real, hence no way to distinguish it from nothingness. To be *actually* present in and *to* the world at all necessarily entails to be *actively* present to others, through self-manifesting action.[28]

It should be obvious—but apparently is not to many philosophers—that this self-manifestation of a being through action reveals to us not only its existence or presence but also its essence or nature—the *kind* of being it is. Every action by its very nature cannot help but be a self-revelation of the *nature* of the agent—i.e., what *kind of actor* it is. If we really analyze it carefully, does not all our knowledge of the so-called essences or inner natures of things really boil down to this: "What is being X? It is *this kind of actor*, or, in more technical terms, it is an abiding active center of power to express itself in such and such characteristic ways." *To be* is *to be an actor*; to know a being is to know *what kind of actor it is*. Is not this what in fact we really want to know about things—not some hidden essence locked in itself apart from any relation to action, but rather the inner capacities of this thing to act, to make a *difference* to the us and to the world?

One of the extremely important consequences of this theory of knowledge through action is that it contains built into it the implication of the always partial relativity, the perspectival character, of our human knowledge (at least in this life). And this for two reasons: (1) an agent may not be able to, or wish to, reveal itself fully in any one action, especially if it is a material agent—and even more so a spiritual agent manifesting itself through a body; and (2) since, according to the ancient adage, often repeated by St. Thomas, what is received is received according to the mode of the receiver, the knower receiving and trying to interpret the action of a being on it may be—and necessarily is, if it is material—restricted by its own limited nature from receiving the full range of the agent's self-manifesting actions, and so in what it can positively affirm with evidence about the being's inner nature or characteristic powers. Thus human knowledge can be certain in what it affirms about the natures of things insofar as they do positively reveal themselves through action to us. But it can never go on to claim that it knows the full essence of the thing in itself. All real beings, including not least our own very selves, are for us human knowers always a shifting blend of known–unknown, of *chiaroscuro*, light and shadow.

The failure to grasp fully, or sometimes to admit at all, this indissoluble link between knowledge and the self-revelation of being through action is to my mind one of the major lacunae that have plagued Western epistemology since Descartes, who first saddled us with the impossible rationalist ideal of a knowledge so absolutely certain that its opposite was logically impossible, an ideal unrealizable in fact—outside of the Cartesian *cogito* (I think, therefore I am). It is in particular the fatal flaw in the entire theory of knowledge of the great Immanuel Kant, who has so inhibited and intimidated philosophers of knowledge since his time, with his solemn dictum "Things as they are in themselves are unknown to us." We know only their appearances in us, structured by our own built-in mental forms and categories. But Kant has locked himself into an insoluble dilemma. On the one hand, he insists that we must posit an outside world of things-in-themselves (or *noumena*), which must first act upon us, since he rejects idealism—we are not total creators of the things we know the way God is, if there is one. On the other hand, he insists with equal vigor that this real world of agents remains totally unknowable to us as it is in itself, providing only an amorphous kind of raw material which we then actively mold into intelligibility by our own *a priori* forms of sense and intellect. Hence we know the world only as it appears to us (*phenomena*). According to his Copernican Revolution in philosophy, it is not the world that informs our knowledge, but our minds that impose our own form and structure on the world. Hence his cardinal philosophical "sin" is to admit that beings *act upon us*, but to deny that such action is *revelatory* of anything at all about these beings, which remain totally opaque—unrevealed—to us.

But this is totally to misconstrue the nature of action. Action is of its very nature self-revelatory to some significant degree of the nature of the agent from which it flows. An action which reveals nothing whatsoever about its agent-source is not action at all. Once he admits the real action of outside things upon us at all—and of course even this he could not with strict consistency allow, since causal action is itself for him only one of our built-in categories of the mind and cannot be projected objectively onto the world in itself—he should have followed through to allow that we know *something* about the *inner natures* (i.e., natural powers) of the agents that act upon us, which manifest themselves through their actions on us.

I suspect that what blocked him was a hang-over of the old rationalist ideal, that to know a thing in itself one would have to know its essence *fully* as it is in itself *apart from* and independent of any action, as the creative mind of God would know it. If we cannot know it this way, then we cannot know it at all. But of course we cannot know the essences of real beings, nor even our own essence, in this purely static way. In fact, even God, St. Thomas would insist, although He does not know His creatures *through* their action as a medium, would still, in order to know their true essences, have to know these essences as abiding centers of natural power *ordered* toward their manifestation through action. For, as he has told us, "Every substance exists for the sake of its operation. . . . Indeed, operation is the ultimate perfection of each thing." As for ourselves, though we cannot grasp the inner essences of things directly in themselves through themselves, we can *point back* to the nature through the intentionality of the act of judgment, which *affirms* on the evidence of a thing's action that there must be and is *in the agent* an inner *power* to manifest itself this way through action. This is a genuine knowledge, through affirmation, of a thing *as it is in itself* as a natural power or source of action, but always indissolubly linked to the manifestation of inner power through characteristic self-revealing action. As St. Thomas himself puts it in a text that always seems to astonish Kantians, "The substantial forms of things, which are unknown to us as they are in themselves, shine forth to us [*innotescunt*] through their accidental properties (i.e., their operations, etc.)." [29] He also adds, "Our knowledge is so weak that no philosopher was ever able to investigate perfectly the nature of a single fly. Hence we read that one philosopher passed thirty years in solitude that he might know the nature of the bee." [30]

Knowledge through action, then, is the key to all human knowledge of the real. But it also allows only a moderate, relational realism, not an absolute intuition of essences in themselves. It should be clear, furthermore, that all our knowledge of God must follow the same rule: we know Him through and only through His self-manifestation in action. Our natural knowledge of God comes from His self-manifestation in the Book of Creation; our supernatural knowledge comes from His self-manifestation in His special salvific actions in human history, as revealed in the Book of Revelation. From all the above it should by now be clear why I consider action and its connection with both being and knowing to be one of the central pillars of reality and our explanation of it, and why I consider the article I have written on this point, "Action as the Self-Revelation of Being: A Central Theme in St. Thomas," one of the most important I have done. [31]

5. *The Good*

The above analysis of action and its natural link with being opens out immediately into the discovery of the good, so that, just as action is woven into the very fabric of being itself, so too is the good woven into the very fabric of action and thereby of being. Being and value are inseparable. The reason is that every action tends necessarily to some goal, some end sought for, consciously or unconsciously. An action that is not focused on any determinate end at all is not a determinate action and hence is not action at all. The intelligibility of any action comes half from behind, from the agent that is its source, and half from ahead, from the goal the action is tending toward. The goal of the action as being tended toward is what is technically called the "final cause," or the end (*finis*) as cause, and the focusing of the action as attracted by the goal is "final causality." Hence the ancient metaphysical adage stemming from Aristotle—but implicit also in Plato—"Every agent acts for an end." Now, as St. Thomas explains it, every goal as sought after or desired, consciously or not, has the character of a *good*—i.e., something sought after as fulfilling, perfecting the agent or another to which the agent wishes fulfillment of some kind. Hence every action by its very nature is *for the good*, dynamically drawn or magnetized by the good. The search for value is woven into the very dynamism of all action, hence of all real being.

There is, however, a shadow or tragic side to this universal quest for the good. Although all action is necessarily drawn toward some good, this good, especially in conscious beings that act through some degree of choice, may be only an *apparent* good, not really fulfilling to the agent at all, or such a limited good that pursuit of it will necessarily exclude the achieving of some higher good that should be present for the genuine overall fulfillment of the agent as a whole. This is the central tragic flaw in every human life and all of human history on the social level, that, blinded by too narrowly self-centered egocentric drives, or even by simple ignorance, we are bewitched by the quest for goods that are either illusory or destructive from a long-range holistic point of view. In a word, our loving is not *wise* loving, in view of the authentic fulfillment of our lives seen as a whole, in the perspective also of the total, unified order of the good for the universe as a whole.

But this tragic possibility of illusion and disorder in our quest for the good does not in the least negate the intrinsic link of all action and hence of all being with the good. Value is intrinsic to being, conceived dynamically, not something added on from the outside (or even projected by the subject alone) onto a base of being seen as sheer brute, value-free fact. Here we part company with so many modern thinkers since Hume, for whom there is a split between being as mere fact and value, which must be added on from without by the subject. No real being can be a mere static fact unrelated to value, but as intrinsically dynamic must of its very nature be value-oriented. Even the celebrated problem of contemporary ethical philosophy, the so-called unbridgeable gap between the "is" and the "ought," can be closed this way, I believe; not on the formal conceptual level, where the two are irreducible, but on the deeper metaphysical level, where one flows naturally into the other. It is to the profound insight of Plato that we first owe, it seems, the discovery (in reflective philosophical terms) of the absolute centrality of the Good. For him nothing can be at all unless it is in some way good—although St. Thomas gently corrects, in view of his own dynamic existential notion of being, Plato's assignment of radical priority to the Good over being, "above and beyond all being and essence," as he says enigmatically in the *Republic* (VI, 509B).

The good, then, suffuses all action and all being itself, and since nothing can be good, for St. Thomas, unless it actually *is* in some way, to be itself becomes the fundamental good. Thus the search for being as the good is the ultimate trigger of all action. And as soon as we reach the higher levels of being, that is, self-conscious being, the notion of the good blossoms out into the notion of *love*, equally ultimate, though not as widely extending as the good. And since the ultimate source of the whole universe must in the last analysis be an intelligent, self-conscious cause, the ultimate secret of the very existence of the universe at all must be an act of love, Infinite Being's love of its own infinite goodness as something not only to be enjoyed by itself, but as something to share with others as its images. As Meister Eckhart put it with dazzling brevity, "God enjoys himself, and wants us to join Him." Thus, too, since all desire for the good is analogously a form of love, it is literally true that, as Dante puts it in the *Paradiso* of his *Divine Comedy*, "Love makes the world go round." The utimate answer to Heidegger's—and before him Leibniz'—question "Why is there anything at all rather than nothing?" is Love. There is no profounder depth in being, no further answer possible. Notice that even the good by itself is not enough; there must also be some loving or desiring subject to

77

seek it actively. The freedom or in some way necessity of this radical, universe-grounding act of love is one of the profoundest and most mysterious problems in metaphysics, which I dare not enter into here. To sum up this whole section: being, action, the good, and love form an inseparable quaternity (which could easily be reduced to a trinity) at the most intimate core of all that is. *To be, ultimately, is to be loved and to love* (though for God the order is reversed).

6. *The Person*

The person for St. Thomas is "that which is most perfect in all of nature."[32] It is an actually existing being possessing a rational nature—i.e., endowed with intellect and will—and considered as an integral whole including all its essential parts. (That is why for him the separated human soul after death, waiting for the resurrection of its co-partner, the body, is not yet properly a person, since existing as an *embodied spirit* is essential to the nature of man as a distinctive mode of being, so that without it our souls do not have their natural integral wholeness in the order of being. Only the body–soul composite is fully and properly a human person; the soul without the body is only "the soul *of* . . . John Jones," etc. This is a strongly anti-Platonic position, by the way.) What is so special about the person that situates it at the apex of the order of being? St. Thomas pinpoints this in what is not only the briefest, but I think one of the most profound, definitions or descriptions of the person ever given. The person, he says, is that which is *dominus sui*,[33] or *master of itself*: that is to say, *self-possessing* of its own being; self-possessing in the order of *knowledge* by its self-consciousness or self-awareness; self-possessing in the order of *action* by its power of self-determination, or free will. It is essentially, though incompletely and imperfectly in man, an *autonomous subject*, knowingly and freely guiding itself in its quest for self-fulfillment through the good, in contrast to lower orders of being, which are not self-guiding but moved by instincts or natural tendencies over which they have no, or a very reduced, control. This does not mean that the human person does not need the world and other persons for its ful-fillment, but that it must relate itself to others knowingly and freely, by its *own* act, in order to reach this fulfillment.

The working-out of the laws of authentic self-development for the person belongs rather to the philosophy of man, and is not our specific concern here as metaphysicians, though it has always interested me very much, and has played a key role in my philosophical reflection and teaching. But the connection of the person with the fullness of being and the dynamic order of the universe as a whole is very much our concern here. It is in this perspective that the notion of person lights up as the perfection of being coming to its full flowering of *self-possessing active presence,* an inner luminous *presence to it-self,* not just to others by its outward oriented actions. Note that to be a person does not imply something else or special added onto being from the outside, as to some more basic, purely objective—as opposed to subjective—impersonal fact or state. Personal being is nothing but being itself, freed from the limits of material modes of existence that hold it down in the darkness of un–self-conscious *lack* of self-presence, being itself allowed now to take on the full dimensions of what it meant to *be,* that is, to be active *presence in the world.*[34] Thus, the fewer the limitations of essence on a being, the more it is able to realize the full "nature" of being as presence, tending toward the ideal fullness, found only in God, of total luminous presence not only to itself but to all other beings—an active power-filled presence with the creative energy to make all others things present. *To be* without restrictions, therefore, necessarily means *to be personal.*

I am well aware that I am here parting company with many of the great Oriental traditions of thought, for which the very notion of person and of personal loving are infected with a relativity and hence limitation that will not allow them to be extended all the way to the Infinite One. But I believe for my part—and I know this would be disputed by Orientals—that this stems partly from a failure to pursue far enough the anal-ysis of analogy.[35] It is indeed true that to apply meaningfully these notions to God we must extend them analogously by dropping off the limitations of our way of experiencing them, then projecting them through causal participation all the way to the profound mystery hidden from our direct conceptual grasp. But I also believe that the result, the hidden term we point toward through the unrestricted dynamism of the mind, is a mystery of light, of super-personal being, rather than the darkness of infra-personal being. This problem, however, one of the most difficult in metaphysics, is too deep for us to discuss further here.

But we can go further. Not only must the ultimate Source of the universe be personalized being, precisely because it is the fullness of active presence, so that the rest of the universe derives *from* personal being; we can also say that for the created universe to make full sense it would have to include personal created beings within it—in a word, it would have to be *for* persons. For without conscious persons in the universe, outside of God there would be no one to be aware of this magnificent gift of being, this self-communication of the divine goodness, no one to appreciate it and give thanks for it. What could possibly be the point of a created universe entirely plunged in the darkness of unconsciousness, unable to know or appreciate that it is there at all? It could hardly be for the sake of God himself, who as infinite plenitude of being is already infinitely rich and needs nothing further to fulfill Him. Thus it would seem to me that we have excellent grounds for affirming that a created universe would be meaningless unless it contained created persons within it, unless it were not only *from* a personal Source but also *for* persons, a gift *to* persons. It would also be true that if the created universe were totally unconscious there would be no way for it to complete its return to God in the Great Circle of Being, as we shall see in a moment when dealing with the universe as Journey. Thus our—and any—universe turns out to be a radically personalized one, in its source, its meaning, and its destiny. Mind and love are at the root of all being. The person is ultimately the key to why there is anything at all and not rather nothing.

Furthermore, the notion of person itself necessarily turns out to be *interpersonal*. There is no "I" without a "Thou," and hence a "We." This intersubjective aspect of personality is not clearly and explicitly developed by St. Thomas (or the ancients either), although it was opened up with astonishing reflective sophistication by a few of the twelfth-century monastic theologians like Richard of St. Victor and William of St. Thierry (as I learned much later).[36] I was introduced to it through my personal contacts with and study of the Existentialist Personalists during my doctoral studies just after the war, in 1947: for example, Gabriel Marcel,[37] Auguste Brunner (my teacher at Jersey),[38] Emmanuel Mounier,[39] Martin Buber,[40] Maurice Nédoncelle,[41] and other Christian Personalists, such as John Macmurray.[42] It is here, by the way, that the Christian Revelation of God as a Triune Personal Being—a Three in One—opens up in a dazzling new way the mystery of God into which philosophy alone could not penetrate further with any assurance, and sheds immense light on the very nature of being and person. For it reveals that the Supreme Being, by an inner necessity of the perfection of being itself, must be *interpersonal*, a Personal "We," rather than a solitary, utterly simple, and nonrelational One. No wonder, then, that human personality also is intrinsically interpersonal, since it is such a lofty image of the divine perfection.

This intersubjective understanding of personhood, involving as it does the reciprocal receiving as well as giving of love in relation to another person, added an original new perspective to my Thomistically grounded philosophy of God, and guided me in my long and fruitful dialogue with process philosophers of God like Lewis Ford and others.[43] With the notion of person and the perfection appropriate to personal being now controlling all the other attributes of God, so that the perfection of God becomes a single unified, holistic field of meaning, with all the attributes adjusting to each other, I was led to soften or tone down somewhat the (to my mind) too rigorous, abstract, and unqualified interpretation of the immutability and infinity of God as developed in St. Thomas' own texts. This adaptation allows God to receive love from His personal creatures (not merely pour out His goodness to them in a one-way self-communication of love), and to be more positively affected by His creation (new joy, etc.) in a way never countenanced by a more traditional Thomistic philosophy of God. Of course I should add that these moves on my part, proposed as a creative reinterpretation of St. Thomas faithful to his basic metaphysical insights, have called forth various demurrers from other contemporary Thomists, including one especially vigorous recent charge of radical betrayal of authentic Thomism, published in the *New Scholasticism*.[44] But I feel that my head, though somewhat bloodied, is still unbowed in this respect.

THE GREAT CIRCLE OF BEING:
THE UNIVERSE AS JOURNEY

We have now made the tour of the five great pillars of reality that seem to me to have been the central and most fruitful themes of my own unified philosophical vision of the world as worked out over fifty years of metaphysical reflection. There are other themes, of course, which I have worked on, and other metaphysicians, even Thomists, might well choose some others as more central. But I have found that I simply cannot do without any of these, and that with them I can generate most of the other positions in my total philosophical vision. Can we now tie together all of these themes into a single synoptic vision? When one tries to do that, I think he will discover— as I did in preparing this address—that the most spontaneous, natural, and effective way of doing so is to shift gears, so to speak, and move from concepts to images. Only an image, it seems, can hold together at once a multiplicity of conceptual analyses in a holistic unity. For this we have to call on our right brain, the locus—according to contemporary brain theory —of non-analytic, holistic descriptions and images.

The image we shall be using is an ancient and natural one, handed down to us by the great metaphysical tradition of Neoplatonism and taken over with relish by St. Thomas. It is that of the universe seen as a great dynamic *circle of being,* and therefore as a *journey,* a great circular *journey*—to link it up with another ancient and powerful archetypal symbol. As both Plotinus and St. Thomas describe it, the inner dynamism of all being moves in a great circle. First there is the *exodus,* or journey outward of all created being from its Infinite Source, the emanation of the Many from the One, as St. Thomas puts it.[45] This outward movement is grounded in God as exercising *efficient causality*—to shift to Aristotelian technical terminology—actively producing out of His own self-diffusive goodness the whole ordered system of multiple, participated, finite beings, the procession of the Many from the One. But no sooner has the outgoing journey begun than it pivots upon itself and starts back on a journey home again to its Source *(reditus),* drawn by the pull of the Good in each being. This pull arises as the inner act of being of each thing pours over into its characteristic goal-oriented action, seeking the fullness of its own perfection (i.e., its appropriate goodness), and drawn to this goodness ultimately, through the channels of participation, by the same Infinite Goodness from which its original act of existence flowed in the first place, but this time as *final cause.* Thus all created beings, as participating in the Divine Goodness in imitation of their Source, are really striving, as St. Thomas puts it in a magnificent run of thought, to imitate and be united to the Divine Goodness as closely as their natures will allow.[46] Just as "all knowers implicitly know God in all that they know," he tells us, so too all actors, desirers, lovers implicitly love God in all that they love or desire.[47]

Thus the Source as Efficient Cause sends the whole universe out from itself on its journey through multiplicity, and at the same time draws it back to itself through the universal pull of the Good, as Final Cause. So the exodus and the return, the leaving home and returning thereto, the way out and the way back, are a journey motif woven into the very ontological structure of every being and thus of the universe itself as a whole.

But there is something very special, in fact indispensable, about the presence of man in this journey of the *material* universe home to its Source. Without the presence of an intelligent being like man somewhere within it, the material universe on its own would remain totally unconscious of this great circle of being, of its being drawn back toward its Source, and of its own secret goal. Without spiritual intelligence and will it could neither recognize God as its goal nor unite itself with Him by love. Only a being endowed with intelligence and will can be united directly with God. Hence the material universe, vast and magnificent though it be, needs a mediator, a bridge-builder between earth and heaven, lest its return journey be aborted. Man is this mediator, standing in the midst of the material universe, arising out of it as a synthesis of matter and spirit, a microcosm imaging the whole in himself, and with the capacity through his intellect and will to understand the whole process, the entire journey and its meaning, to gather together into his consciousness the entire community of existents, especially the material ones that cannot do this for themselves, and refer them back again with conscious recognition, gratitude, and love to their Source. Thus man takes all of nature with him, so to speak, on his own personal return toward final transforming union with the Infinite Source of his own and of all other being.

Hence man is not supposed to be absorbed merely with his own individual return to God. He has a fundamental job to do, a service to perform, in and for the whole material universe, as the necessary mediator without which it could not complete its own journey back to its Source. The Great Circle of Being would be incomplete, for the material universe, without him. Hence the great dignity, the lofty role of the human person, the whole human race, in this vast cosmos given to us in stewardship. (This, by the way, is one of the great services that contemplative religious orders—apparently, to the outward eye, doing nothing for the common good—can do *for the world*: to gather up in their reflective prayerful consciousness the meaning of the Great Circle of Being, and by their adoration, gratitude, and love complete the return to its Source of a universe that is for the most part all too oblivious of the meaning of its journey or the nature of its Goal.)

The image of journey I have used to gather up the whole meaning of the universe into unity is one of my favorite ones. One reason is the deep archetypal roots that it has in our psyche and in the whole history of art and culture. The theme of the journey, of leaving home and finding one's way home again, is a central one in so many of the great epic poems, novels, plays, etc.[48] And as one of my students, Christina Hinck, who has been of great help to me in calling my attention to illustrations of the journey theme in literature and art, had pointed out to me just before this lecture, even great music so often follows what might be called a circular-journey pattern: it starts off with a theme, then leaves home, so to speak, to develop the theme through many variations, and finally comes back home again by returning in an enriched way to the original theme. Carl Jung, too, lays great stress on the symbol of the journey theme to describe the development of the psyche toward full integration: we must leave home—unconscious primordial oneness with the parents—to affirm and develop our distinct self-identity on our own, but then around midlife begin the journey home again to reintegrate our individuality with our original roots deep in the archetypal unconscious.

This age-old theme of the journey as a symbol of human life is so familiar to us and has so much meaning in our ordinary lives, and yet it has much deeper and more mysterious undertones of resonance with something far larger than our individual lives, that is, with the very hidden life of the universe itself, in whose vast ongoing journey our own is caught up as a reflection. No wonder that the image of journey strikes such deep chords within us; the very structure of being itself involves a journey, a journey of the finite from the Infinite and back to the Infinite. And the latest work in physics and cosmology only confirms this, since the Big Bang Theory of the origin of the material universe now reveals that the entire cosmos from the first fiery moment of its origin to the present is enveloped in a single great unified journey. Physics and metaphysics here reinforce each other. And the spiritual journey of each one of us becomes a microcosm of the larger journey.

Before bringing my reflections to a close, I feel I should take brief notice of an important challenge brought up in the discussion after the original address. The metaphysical picture of the universe that I have painted so far seems a very optimistic one, where all is in order in the great journey. But how does all the evil and darkness that is so obvious in the universe fit into this bright picture? My answer is very simple: I have not developed that aspect here, but it certainly can and should be done. Does not the very notion of journey imply risk, adventure, the possibility of losing one's way, of wandering off the path, either deliberately or unwittingly, of getting lost, possibly even permanently? As realized in the concrete, existential, contingent world, it certainly does. This has always been part of the great symbolic depictions of the *human* journey, at least. Although it is my conviction that more light can be shed on this shadow aspect of the Great Circle of Being than is commonly believed, it must ultimately remain a mystery whose depths cannot be plumbed by us in our present state of wayfarers. As St. Augustine put it, "To try to understand evil is like trying to hear silence or see darkness." But I also believe—and would love to show you if I had the time— that all philosophical attempts to turn this shadow and mystery dimension into a cogent *objection* against the goodness of God or the meaningfulness of the universe can be shown by careful analysis to be infected with insurmountable logical and conceptual mistakes. The inevitable *chiaroscuro*, light-

and-shadow, pattern of the universe still remains decisively more light than shadow, even taking into account the great modern "Masters of Suspicion," as they have been called: Nietzsche, Freud, Marx, possibly even Derrida and the Deconstructionists—i.e., if one considers the latter's thought to be more than a merely ephemeral excursion.[49]

I must now bring to a close my own journey back over fifty years of metaphysical reflection. I would like this image of the Great Circle of Being, the universe as a journey, to be the last word in my own metaphysical pilgrimage of trying to understand all being in an integrated synoptic vision, and my own place within this larger journey. I can only wish that all of you who read this may have some share in the deeply satisfying, yet inexhaustibly mystery-filled, wonder and profound joy of spirit I have found in my own journey.[50]

NOTES

1. For a summary of his thought, see F. O'Farrell, s.j., "The Dialectic of the Affirmation by Fr. André Marc, s.j.," *Gregorianum*, 35 (1954), 474–91; F. Fontan, "L'Itinéraire intérieur du Père André Marc," *Archives de Philosophie*, 28 (1965), 180–205.

2. Etienne Gilson, *Le Thomisme*, 5th ed. (Paris, 1945); trans. *The Christian Philosophy of St. Thomas Aquinas* (New York: Random House, 1956); Joseph de Finance, s.j., *Être et agir* (Paris: Beauchesne, 1945). See also Helen James John, "The Emergence of the Act of Existing in Recent Thomism," *International Philosophical Quarterly*, 2 (1962), 600–25.

3. L.-B. Geiger, *La Participation dans la philosophie de s. Thomas d'Aquin* (Paris, 1945); C. Fabro, *La Nozione metafisica di partecipazione secondo s. Tommaso d'Aquino* (Turin: Società Editrice Internazionale, 1945); J. de Finance, *Être et agir*.

4. *Capax entis*: with a capacity for being; *potens omnia fieri*: with the potentiality to become all things.

5. See Chapter I of my *The Philosophical Approach to God: A Neo-Thomist Perspective* (Winston-Salem: Wake Forest University, 1979).

6. See my "What Is Really Real?" in *Progress in Philosophy*, ed.

J. McWilliams (Milwaukee: Bruce, 1955), pp. 61–90, together with the attack on it, by James Conway, s.j., "The Reality of the Possibles," *New Scholasticism*, 33 (1959), 139–61, 331–53, and my reply, "The Possibles Revisited," ibid., 34 (1960), 79–102. The same existential theme recurs in most of my articles on St. Thomas.

7. Martin Heidegger, *Was ist Metaphysik?* (Bonn: Cohen, 1930), p. 173.

8. In his "Essay on Life," in *Shelley's Prose*, ed. D. L. Clark (Albuquerque: University of New Mexico Press, 1954), p. 172.

9. Marcel de Corte, *La Philosophie de Gabriel Marcel* (Paris: Tequi, 1937), p. 74.

10. Poets have often been sensitive to this. See, for example, Coleridge, *The Friend*, III, 192, quoted by Dorothy Emmet, "Some Questions to a Modern Thomist," *Theology*, 52 (1949), 456n1: "Hast thou ever raised thy mind to the consideration of existence, in and by itself, as the mere act of existing? Hast thou ever said to thyself thoughtfully, It is! Heedless in that moment, whether it were a man before thee, or a flower, or a grain of sand,—without reference, in short, to this or that particular mode or form of existence? If thou hast indeed attained to this, thou wilt have felt the presence of a mystery, which must have fixed thy spirit with awe and wonder."

11. "Ipsa actualitas rei est quasi lumen ipsius," *Super librum De causis expositio*, ed. Saffrey (Fribourg, 1954), Cap. 1, lect. 6.

12. A useful summary of the points in St. Thomas' metaphysics of most abiding value can be found in my article for the seventh centenary of his death, "What Is Most and Least Relevant in St. Thomas' Metaphysics Today?," *International Philosophical Quarterly*, 14 (1974), 411–34.

13. See the works mentioned in n. 3. For a fine example of a systematic treatise of Thomistic metaphysics built around the participation doctrine, see L. De Raeymaeker, *La Philosophie de l'être* (Louvain: Editions de l'Institut Supérieur de Philosophie, 1947); trans. *The Philosophy of Being* (St. Louis: Herder, 1954). See also my own articles that had considerable influence in introducing the doctrine to English-speaking readers: "The Limitation of Act by Potency: Aristotelianism or Neoplatonism?," *New Scholasticism*, 26 (1952), 167–94; "The Meaning of Participation in St. Thomas," *Proceedings of the American Catholic Philosophical Association*, 26 (1952), 147–57.

14. Henri Bergson, "Philosophical Intuition," in *The Creative Mind* (New York: Philosophical Library, 1946), p. 128.

15. This sense of the underlying affinity of all things, as belonging to the universe of being, is beautifully expressed by Gabriel Marcel in his *Mystery of Being* (Chicago: Gateway, 1966), I, 19: "I have laid such stress on intersubjectivity precisely because I wish to emphasize the presence of an underlying reality that is felt, of a community that is deeply rooted in ontology; without this, human relations, in any real sense, would be unintelligible. . . . In more concrete language: I concern myself with being only insofar as I have a more or less distinct consciousness of the underlying unity which ties me to other beings of whose reality I have a preliminary notion."

16. See the fine statement of this by Stephen Brown, s.j., *The World of Imagery* (London, 1927), pp. 17–18: "In its most characteristic and distinctive form it [the metaphorical mode of intelligence] is a using of material objects as images of immaterial, spiritual things. It is founded on the existence of analogies and correspondences between the various objects or phenomena of nature, and between these again and human life—man's emotional, moral, and intellectual nature, between matter and mind. Imagery is a witness to the harmony of mind and matter, to the unity of all creation, and thus to the oneness of its author." See also Caroline Spurgeon, *Shakespeare's Imagery and What It Tells Us* (New York: Macmillan, 1936), p. 7: "For I believe that analogy—likeness between dissimilar things—which is the fact underlying the possibility and reality of metaphor, holds within itself the very secret of the universe. . . ."

17. See my own fuller exposition of this whole metaphysical ascent to God in St. Thomas in *The Philosophical Approach to God*, Chap. II.

18. See my fuller development in "Action as the Self-Revelation of Being: A Central Theme in St. Thomas," in *The History of Philosophy in the Making*, ed. Linus Thro (Washington: University Press of America, 1982), pp. 62–80.

19. *De Potentia*, q. 2, art. 1.

20. *Summa contra Gentes*, I, 43.

21. *Scriptum super libris Sententiarum*, Lib. I, dist. 4, q. 1, art. 1.

22. *Summa contra Gentes*, II, 66.

23. *Expositio in lib. De anima*, Lib. II, lect. 5, n. 281.

24. *Summa contra Gentes*, III, 113.

25. *Summa Theologiae*, I, q. 76, art. 1.

26. *Summa contra Gentes*, II, 79.

27. *Summa Theologiae*, I, q. 77, art. 1, ad 7um.

28. I cannot resist quoting here what I consider the great metaphysical poem of Gerard Manley Hopkins, Poem no. 57 in *Poems of Gerard Manley Hopkins* (London: Oxford University Press, 1948), p. 95:

As kingfishers catch fire, dragonflies draw flame;
As tumbled over rim in roundy wells
Stones ring; like each tucked string tells, each hung bell's
Bow swung finds tongue to fling out broad its name;
Each mortal thing does one thing and the same;
Deals out that being indoors each one dwells;
Selves—goes itself; *myself* it speaks and spells;
Crying *what I do is me: for that I came.*

I say more: the just man justices;
Keeps grace: that keeps all his goings graces;
Acts in God's eye what in God's eye he is—
Christ—for Christ plays in ten thousand places,
Lovely in limbs, and lovely in eyes not his
To the Father through the features of men's faces.

29. See text quoted in n. 27.

30. *Collationes super Credo in Deum*, in *Opuscula Theologica* II (Rome: Marietti, 1954).

31. See n. 17; also, for action through dialogue as the key to realistic epistemology, especially against Kant, my "Interpersonal Dialogue as the Key to Realism," in *Person and Community*, ed. Robert J. Roth, s.j. (New York: Fordham University Press, 1975), pp. 141–54.

32. *Summa Theologiae*, I, q. 29, art. 3.

33. *Summa Theologiae*, I–II, q. 6, art. 2, ad 2m; II–II, q. 64, art. 5, ad 3m; *De Veritate*, q. 5, art. 10.

34. See Karl Rahner, *Spirit in the World* (New York: Herder & Herder, 1968).

35. I develop this more fully in my *The Philosophical Approach to God*, Chap. II; also in my longer article, "Analogy and the

Meaningfulness of Language about God," *Thomist*, 40 (1976), 61–95.

36. I discovered this while directing two Ph.D. dissertations: Ewert Cousins, "The Notion of the Person in the *De Trinitate* of Richard of St. Victor" (Fordham University, 1966), and Thomas Tomasic, "William of St. Thierry: Toward a Philosophy of Inter-subjectivity" (Fordham University, 1972).

37. For a fine synthesis, see Arthur Luther, "Marcel's Meta-physics of the We Are," *Philosophy Today*, 10 (1966), 190–203.

38. *La Personne incarnée* (Paris: Beauchesne, 1947).

39. *Personalism* (Notre Dame: University of Notre Dame Press, 1952).

40. *I and Thou*, rev. ed. (New York: Scribners, 1961).

41. *Vers une philosophie de l'amour et de la personne* (Paris: Aubier, 1948).

42. I have been deeply influenced by the two seminal books of John Macmurray, *The Self as Agent* and *Persons in Relation* (London: Faber & Faber, 1961 & 1962), forming together his Gif-ford Lectures, The Form of the Personal.

43. See my *A Philosophical Approach to God*, Chap. III, de-voted entirely to this question.

44. Theodore Kondoleon, "The Immutability of God: Some Recent Challenges," *New Scholasticism*, 58 (1984), 293–315.

45. The entire *Summa Theologiae* is built on this pattern of the emanation of all creatures from God and their return to Him through man and Christ. Part One deals with "the emanation of all being from God"; Parts Two and Three, with the *reditus* or return. For a synthetic exposé of the Great Circle in terms of inten-tionality, see André Hayen, "L'Intentionalité de l'être et méta-physique de la participation," *Revue Néoscolastique de la Philo-sophie*, 42 (1939), 385–410; St. Thomas, *In I Sententiarum*, d. 14, q. 2, a. 2.

46. *Summa contra Gentes*, III, 16–21; also I, 19; II, 20.

47. *De Veritate*, q. 22, art. 2, ad 1um.

48. The summer seminars sponsored by the National Endow-ment for the Humanities and conducted by Dr. Ewert Cousins of the Fordham University Department of Theology on the "Journey Theme" in medieval thought and literature bear eloquent witness to this.

49. For a remarkably clear exposition of the negative thrust of the Deconstructionist analysis as regards metaphysics, see Briankle Chiang, "The Eclipse of Being: Heidegger and Derrida," *International Philosophical Quarterly*, 15 (1985), 113–38.

50. If we add on to our metaphysical reflection the light of Christian Revelation, a new dimension is added to the journey by the entrance of God himself into it in the man Jesus to share and transform it.

Being and the Mystery of the Person

John D. Caputo
Villanova University

HEIDEGGER SAYS THAT THINKING IS THANKING, by which he means that thinking comes in response to the graciousness of Being. Let us say that in these remarks thanking will take the form of thinking, that we offer to Norris Clarke, in gratitude for a lifetime of illumination and insight, an exercise in thinking, a work of thought in thanks for a life of thinking.

I want to think here the question of the person. Such thinking might be called "phenomenological" because it knows no other way to proceed than by the closest heeding of the structure of lived experience, and "hermeneutic" because it recognizes the unavoidability of interpretation, that there is no sheer beholding of unambiguous structures. Indeed, thinking turns on the notion of ambiguity, of undecidability, of a certain labyrinthine circumstance in which we are all implicated, like it or not. It might also be called "ontological," because I take the person to be a privileged point of departure for the question of Being. Finally, such thinking might be called "ethical," because for it all of the issues in a philosophical ethic are concentrated in the person.

I want to organize these reflections around the oldest and most literal idea about the person: the person as *per-sonare*—to sound through the mask, to fill the mask with sound, to resound. *Per-sona*: the voice sounding through the mask, the false face placed over the true. *Persona* implies a dialectic between face and hiddenness, an interplay between the mask and what is masked, between concealment and what emerges into unconcealment. Concealment and unconcealment, what Heidegger called ἀλήθεια, is here conceived—beyond Heidegger's intentions—in terms of the *persona*, in terms of face and sub-face. I want to do here something which Heidegger strangely left undone, to tend to a field he strangely left uncultivated, to follow the dialectic of ἀ-λήθεια, of concealment and unconcealment, insofar as it is at work in the person. And what could be more natural, when the very word *per-sona* suggests that the surface is always disturbed by the concealed depths, that the face is always more than sur-face, is always a *plus ultra*, something more? The very word *persona* tells us that something more is resonating through it.

The face—and let us call this my "thesis," if that is an appropriate way to speak here—is a place of transcendence, by which I mean a place in which the transcendent breaks through, and in which we are initiated into deeper things, drawn into the mystery of self, of world, of God. Carried out carefully enough, this hermeneutic phenomenology of the face reveals the mystery (what Heidegger would call the λήθη), by which we are inhabited and in which I want to locate the essential quality of the person. *Persona*: that means for me the being in which mystery resonates, the being defined by its openness to the mystery. The face leads us into the desert, and, by opening up the play of concealment and un-concealment, of masked and un-masked, which is the age-old sense of per-sona, is a worthy matter for "thinking."[1]

And my question is, what is sounding through the mask? What voice do we hear? What sounds and resounds through the face? Is it only a human voice? But that is an altogether strange question to ask. For surely common sense prescribes that it is the human person who speaks, a human voice that resonates through the face. But must we let common sense have the final word? Is it common sense that decides matters of thought? Is it possible to ask whether anyone or anything other than man is sounding through, filling the mask with sound? Can we ask such a question? Were it not a human voice, what then? A divine voice? The voice of God calling us to himself? Or some cosmic voice, and hence less a voice than a certain cosmic rumble or resonating? Is the person a place where something divine sounds through, or something cosmic and mundane? The questioning is odd and it is difficult even to know how to pose it. Might it be indeed that we are led by this exercise in thinking, not so much to answer these questions as to learn how to ask them? Questioning is the piety of thought and the openness to the mystery. Questioning leads us into transcendence, to the breakthrough, exposing us to the λήθη, undermining our assurances. Perhaps the most to ask for in what follows is to learn to ask these questions, that is to say, to learn to think.

KANT AND CLARKE

Norris Clarke has probed the question of the person on a number of occasions and with impressive results.[2] He frequently and rightly takes Kant to task for failing to provide an adequate epistemological ground for our knowledge of the other person, and he rightly argues that, had he done so, Kant would have landed himself on the other side of his transcendental idealism in some form of realism. The one place where the phenomenality of appearance is surpassed, where there can be no doubt about the trans-phenomenality of what is other, is the reality of the other person. The experience of interpersonal dialogue is the best warrant of the claim of realism. In hearing the voice of the other there can be no question of imposing my own forms upon a raw matter. On the contrary, I am addressed by what is genuinely other.

Now, there is a metaphysics at work here, as there is everywhere in Father Clarke's work, which turns on the Thomistic principle *agere sequitur esse*. I translate: Being (*esse*) is manifest, unconcealed, in and through action (*agere*). The Being of the other person is manifest in his discourse because, more generally, action is always a revelation of Being. It belongs to the fecundity of Being, to its self-diffusiveness, to flow over

95

into manifestness. And man is the being who, as Father Clarke writes, "is placed in the midst of the material cosmos with the ability to receive the self-imaging messages of all the material beings around him. . . . It is man's destiny, written into him by the very structure of his nature, to be the one to listen to being, as it reveals itself to him. . . ."[3] Every being is a *persona* of a certain sort, an actor that speaks to us through its action, whose action manifests its Being to us, a being through which Being sounds.

The other person is delivered to us, not immediately, but through the mediation of his action and language. We make contact, but not naked contact. And it is just this self-revelatory dimension of Being which is denied in Kant's epistemology. Because he thinks that Being manages to act upon me while altogether concealing itself, Kant effectively denies the principle *agere sequitur esse*. The influence that things exert upon us is extinguished by the active domination of them by our consciousness. But in the eminently balanced view of moderate realism, things both reveal and conceal themselves to us. Hence it is *esse, esse reale*, real Being, which resonates through the *per-sona* for Father Clarke.

Now, I have no wish to rush to the defense of Kant on this point. I am content to let him twist slowly in the wind of Father Clarke's critique. I agree that Kant has no good epistemological theory of how the other person is given to us. But I do want to point out that, while Kant lacked an epistemology of the person, he insisted upon a certain moral faith in the existence of others as the matter of conscience, the material object of the law. The other was for him a kind of fourth postulate of practical reason, an object of practical faith. Whence to understand Kant's account of other persons we would need to look, not to Kant's epistemology, but to his ethics, not to the *personalitas transcendentalis*, but to the *personalitas moralis*.

In the second and third formulations of the categorical imperative, which command the will to treat the other as an end in itself, and hence with the same respect that is deserved by the law itself, Kant makes it clear that the moral agent belongs to a community of agents to whom he is bound in conscience. Every rational being is a being capable of moral action, of rising above and asserting himself to be more than a piece of nature, and hence worthy to be treated as an end in himself. The person enjoys a worth or dignity (*Würde*) that arises from his power to act in ways which are inherently worthy of respect—to keep promises faithfully, to be benevolent in principle. Through the person the law enters the world and acquires concrete form. We feel the power of law pulsating through the other. What resonates, what sounds through the *per-sona* for Kant, is the unconditional authority of the law. The rational being is the law itself, if not on horseback, at least in the flesh, in person, in the person. In Kant's own ponderous formulation, the law is "schematized" by the concrete person in whom we see the law at work.

It seems to me that there is something essentially right in all this, but that Kant's formulations are vitiated by his Enlightenment frame of mind and his dualist metaphysics. And it seems to me likewise that with a slight wave of the phenomenological wand one can cash in Kant's claims for experiential coin.[4] We all know of Kant's beginnings, of his pietist home, and of the tender regard with which he held the men and women of his childhood who led decent but humble, virtuous but obscure lives. The humblest servant is the equal of any man of means, Kant thought, when it comes to uprightness of will. Kant was moved by these examples of moral excellence to a lifelong and unshakable belief in the dignity of people of common decency. His analysis of the feeling of respect—which, I believe, his own dualism makes impossible—is, as Heidegger says, a rich phenomenological description of moral feeling. Kant's ethics originates in a deep and lasting experience of the other person.[5]

But to take this experience seriously would, as Norris Clarke argues, provoke a serious upheaval in Kant's epistemology and, as I want to argue, an equally serious upheaval in his ethics. For even in the ethics Kant takes the person, not in his naked humanness, but rather as the embodiment of the law. In the remainder of this paper I want to take the experience of the other seriously and so to till the phenomenological soil from which Kant's own moral experience of the other arises. I want to ask once again: what is the *Being* of the person? What is sounding through and resonating in the *per-sona*?

To do this, I want to take up the question of the face.

<hr>

THE FACE AND THE MYSTERY OF THE OTHER

Let us attend to the phenomenon of the face, and with phenomenological attentiveness. What does it give us to think? What is at play in the face, in the interplay between face and depth, sur-face and sub-face? The face is a surface which reveals and conceals, which is filled with hidden forces, which is always something *more* than it gives itself out to be. What is this something more? What secrets does it harbor—and betray? What powers and forces resonate here?

To discuss these questions I want to rethink two phenomena which Kant discussed—the analysis of lying and the treatment of the feeling of respect—in terms of a phenomenology of the face. The work of *deception* and the right to *respect*. What do they have to do with the face? Or with each other? Do they have a common source, draw upon the same reserves? What do they say about *per-sona*, about what we call here the mystery of the other?

Lying. Lying is a good example for Kant of a maxim whose universalization results in self-contradiction. But let us consider it here, not in relation to the law, but in relation to the face. Let us see if the contradiction in which it is implicated is more than logical. Let us see if lying does not point to a deeper division in our nature.

Language, which is the bearer of truth, is centered in the face. Language is seated in the *lingua*, in the tongue, mouth, lips, and it is overseen by the eyes. Language is *lingua, labia, facies.* To speak is not merely to utter words or to form propositions. It is to orchestrate an entire concert by means of which one's words are supported by an ensemble of facial and bodily accompaniments. A merriness in the eyes, a sadness around the lips, clenched teeth, cold looks—all give the fragile sequence of signs its power to convince, to persuade, to have an effect. Speech acts are acts, acting, performances of a *dramatis persona* whose effect is to persuade an audience.

But this gestural accompaniment is for the most part non-intentionalistic, pre-conceptual, para-linguistic. We do not control this ensemble of gesture and expression—and that is why Husserl did not consider it language properly so-called.[6] Indeed what is harder than *trying* to smile for a camera or *trying* to look surprised? The support the body lends to discourse arises spontaneously. The face is a field of implicit and unthematic operations. An eyebrow pronounces wordless contempt; a spontaneous smile, without premeditation, declares that approval has been won. One's whole being-in-the-world is disclosed without the intervention of conscious control. And it is precisely because the face escapes the monitoring of the ego that language can be so profoundly ambiguous. I can say with my eyes that I want something very badly, even though my words say I do not want it at all. A poorly concealed look of pain says that I have been bitterly disappointed, even though "I" say with my words that it does not matter at all. There is fear on the face, even when one's words are brave; anger, even when one speaks softly.

But it is just because the face is a play of surfaces that we can become adept at lying, which is in this view a peculiarly deep and illustrative disruption of our being-in-the-world. The "cold liar" is, from the point of view of a phenomenology of the face, a frightening phenomenon, an enormously divided and rent being. He stares us in the eyes yet dissembles. He seems to have acquired the power to interrupt this whole system of communication between the body and the face, on the one hand, and spoken discourse, on the other. He has acquired the diabolic art of silencing the bodily system, of trafficking in words that do not arise from fundamental projects. He is able to orchestrate his words with a bodily and facial accompaniment that is pure artifact. He is a master-mime with an unnatural control over his body. He is able to keep his eyes from betraying him, to bring all the clues and signals, all the minute and unconscious indications that are alive in the face, under conscious control. He tries to acquire total domination over his body.

The inconsistency of lying was a favorite example of Kant's. But this inconsistency is not, as Kant thought, a purely logical matter of non-universalizability. In fact, from a merely logical point of view, it can be quite consistently carried out, not only with others but even with oneself. If it were only a matter of logic, we could do it. If all we had to contend with were the first formulation of the categorical imperative, we could get away with it. The inconsistency of lying, however, cuts deeper than logic; it is a bodily matter which can be grasped, not in logical, but only in phenomenological terms. Lying puts us at odds with our most implicit and tacit gestural life, demands that we be ever on guard against the slightest hint of betrayal, that there never be a moment when we are caught off-guard. It demands total domination of our bodily being-in-the-world, that nothing be left tacit, implicit, pre-conscious, inadvertent, unguarded. It demands absolute consciousness and a lived dualism between consciousness and body. Indeed, one would even have to keep one's dreams secret. Lying demands absolute vigilance.

Lying exploits the face as a play of surfaces and the performance of a *dramatis persona*. Lying trades on the interplay between sur-face and concealment, manifest and latent. In lying—and this is what interests us here—we are brought up short against the capacity of the other to hold himself back, to keep himself in reserve, to hide himself behind images of his own creation. Lying discloses the thickness and opacity of language and its power to serve as a veil through which the other withdraws even as he discloses himself. We do not make immediate contact with the other. We have no firm grasp of who it is that looks out at us through those eyes, who is speaking, smiling, appearing to be delighted at our arrival. We are all more or less adept at the art of self-concealment; we all know how to don the mask.

Indeed, even when we suppose that we speak with perfect honesty, we cannot avoid this self-concealment and self-with-drawal. If lying is a case of intentionally suppressing our beliefs, we ought not to suppose that there is some state of absolute self-contact, of perfect self-transparency, where we keep in perfect touch with ourselves. On the contrary, we maintain, it belongs to the ontological make-up of the person to keep slipping away. It belongs to the a-lethic make-up of the person that the element of λήθη is ineradicable. For, quite apart from whatever is intentionally suppressed in lying, there is the vast realm of what is unconsciously repressed. So that when we speak in good faith, in perfect honesty, we cannot know what or whether "it" (es) says within us, what re-pressed desire speaks without our conscious ex-pression.[7] Then we do not lie to the other, which is the simpler case, but we lie to ourselves, which is more complicated. In either case, lying is ontologically significant and points to the alethic mystery of the self.

Respect. And with that conclusion we are led to the second point in the Kantian analysis which we want to rethink along phenomenological lines, viz., the feeling of respect. We recall that for Kant the person is the place where the law enters the world and acquires mundane form. The law, and hence the person in whom the law is embodied, requires absolute respect. But we ask: is the person the embodiment of the law, or is the law simply a distillation, a way of writing in shorthand our experience of the person? Again, it is the face that will serve as our clue.

The face is the seat, not only of truthfulness and deception, but also of what I want to call here "inviolability." The face commands and forbids. It is the face that places the mark of inviolability upon us, which commands respect and forbids violence.[8] The face cries out against manipulation and subjugation. It is the face of the innocent that speaks the most eloquently for social justice: the face of the starving child, with his deathly stare. It is only if we can see the face of our victims that we can understand that they exist as ends and never as means. The face of the other marks him as an end-in-itself, protests against exploitation, manipulation. Every attempt at objectifying the other—from pornography to murder—must be conceived as an attempt to erase the face of the other. Objectification is possible only to the extent that we can deny and nullify his face.

It is the face that condemns murder. When we place a mask on the criminal to be executed, who is being shielded from whom? Is the condemned spared the sight of his executioner? Or is the executioner spared the horror of the eyes and the look of the condemned? What would it be like were this event to take place face-to-face? Would we find anyone willing to do it? And if we did, would we be cultivating a new breed of professionalized brutality? Were the executioners of Auschwitz watching the faces?

All the commandments directed toward our neighbor issue from the face. Kant was not wrong, he simply had recourse to the wrong organon. He needed a phenomenology of the eyes of the other, not a table of logical judgments and their categorical forms. The person is thus not an instance of the law, or the embodiment of the law; rather, the law arises from the person, the law is issued by the face of the other. It is the eyes of the other that issue the categorical imperative. Indeed, the very word "respect" belongs to an "ocular" metaphysics: the a-spect—the look of the other—commands our re-spect: the way we look back. "Respect"—and this is so not only in the Latinate forms, but also in the German *achten*—means the regard, the look, which we give back or return to those whose look brings us up short. From the eyes of the other comes the look that commands our attention, our attentiveness, our regard.

We thus move beyond all value-theory in this phenomenology of the face. The face of the other is not a value posited by the will, but a command that issues from the hidden depths of the other. The modern notion of value must be deconstructed back into its Greek sense of ἀξιόω, of that which is esteemed, respected, because of the respect it commands. We do not posit values, but things of imposing stature and imposing dignity command our respect.[9]

But what is it about the other that commands our respect? What spell does he cast over us? What power does he exert on us? The answer to that question turns on the ontology of the face. The face is *facies*, sur-face, appearance, phenomenon. But it is the surface which is never mere surface, which always intimates more than it shows. The face is the surface which harbors something hidden, which is inhabited by deeper motives and concealed sense. The essence of the face is to be at one and the same time self-showing and self-concealing, closure and disclosure, in accordance with the ontology of ἀ-λήθεια. The sur-face of the face is to be all writing and sign, a code we can only partly make out, a script of ambiguous messages. Thus the face of the other brings us up short because we know that he knows more than he says, that he says other than he knows, that as often as not he does not know what he says or whence it issues. We know that we have to do here with powers which elude our control, and that is why they command our respect.

The self-withdrawing of the other is the seat of his mystery. It is just this self-withdrawing mystery which gives the person the authority of law, which endows him with the power to command respect and to declare himself inviolable. We are persuaded that we have to do here with powers which elude us and which demand to be recognized. He exerts upon us the power of the unknown. He has the advantage of being a mystery to us. He is like a person who wears dark glasses and who puts us at the awful disadvantage of not being able to see his eyes. The inviolability of the other arises from his inaccessibility, from the limits of our access to him and of his own access to himself. His inaccessibility is the effect, not merely of perversity, as in the simple case of the lie, but of the ineradicable recessiveness of his being, from others and from himself. The face of the other is a constant reminder of the limits of our reach and of the depths of his being, depths we can only partly probe. He draws himself into a circle which can be only partially penetrated by him as well as by us. His words and gestures communicate with us from a source of which we all have only an imperfect, uncertain grasp.

I am not saying that we are forever cut off from him, but that this being with whom we are always and already, from the start, is always in part withheld from us. The intimacy of our presence with him, our being-with, is always qualified by his mysterious reserve. The other is both surface and depth, both access and recess, revelation and concealment. The other holds himself back, is in continual and necessary withdrawal, even in his very commerce with us. His giving of himself—and not only to us but also to himself—is likewise a holding-back.

Thus both analyses—of lying and respect—on our phenomenological account lead curiously to the same result. They both turn on the phenomenon of the self-withdrawing nature of the other. The person is capable of deception (and this includes self-deception) only because of a deeper and more radical trait, the ontological necessity with which his being holds itself back even in the act of giving and self-revelation. Deception and respect have the same root. Both spring from the self-withdrawing center which defines the other, which constitutes his otherness, and which makes the rest of us a reader of signs.

Thus the Thomist principle which Norris Clarke justly invokes, *agere sequitur esse*—what the other does flows from what he is—also implies that *esse* does not give itself immediately, that it is always held in reserve, that *agere* never succeeds in exposing or exhausting *esse*. *Agere* follows upon *esse* but it never quite succeeds in catching up to *esse*, in unfolding it, in being a match for it. *Esse* remains behind, in concealment, even in the very un-concealment of *agere*. The action of God in the production of the world does not exhaust or wholly display the Being of God. The action of any finite agent remains an imperfect exhibition of its Being. If action is the self-revelation of Being, and the refutation of any solipsism, as it is, it is also the self-concealment. Indeed, this self-concealment is as much a testimony to the reality of the other—which is the point which Father Clarke wants to make against Kant—as is his self-revelation in action, for self-concealment too bears witness to depths we cannot plumb, to a reality upon which we cannot lay hands. Being is self-concealing even in its very act of self-revealing. *Agere* springs from a hidden and mysterious root.

We have thus reached a preliminary result in terms of our original and quite odd question: what is sounding and re-sounding through the human *per-sona*? On this phenomenological reading the person resonates with ambiguity and mystery, with a depth which neither he nor we can fathom. The mystery of the face is to be a surface over an abyss. Something deep is playing itself out, something mysterious reveals and conceals itself in the eyes and lips, in the look of pain and the look of joy. What do we see there? What voice is resonating there?

SUFFERING AND THE MYSTERY OF THE PERSON

In speaking of the way the soul makes its way beyond the "names" of God, and exposes itself to the transcendent mystery of the "naked Godhead," Meister Eckhart used the term "breakthrough." In the breakthrough the soul enters what Eckhart called the "abyss" of God, the "desert" where the capacity to name God withers away. And, corresponding to the abyss in God, Eckhart spoke of the abyss within the soul, the deep spot in the soul, deeper than the explicit faculties of intellect and will, where the soul is joined to God. The abyss of God is encountered in the abyss of the soul. *Abyssus abyssum invocat.*

Now, without involving us in a religious mysticism I too would like to speak of a fine point of the soul, where we break through to a similar kind of mysterious depth or desert terrain which we find within ourselves. It is here, in this desert place, this deep ground, that we can make an approach to the

question of what is sounding and resounding in the human
per-sona. To this end I want to extend my analysis of the face
by turning to the face of the one who suffers. What is the look
of suffering? What powers resonate here? Of what mysteries
does it speak? What secrets does it harbor? What concealed
depths do we catch sight of in the eyes of the sufferer?

"Suffering" implies *passivity*; it means that we undergo
something, are subjected to something, against our will, are
invaded by alien powers, subdued by a hostile force. In suffering, we are at the mercy of a power, caught in its grip, and we
can at best bear up under it with dignity—lest we lose our
dignity altogether. We have the power, not to dominate it,
but only to undergo it with dignity. Suffering is *violation*. If
the essence of the person is his inviolability, suffering assaults
and violates him. If we conceive the person in terms of respect,
suffering is a reckless, ravaging invader, which respects no one
and nothing, neither age nor wealth, neither virtue nor power.
Suffering is a transgression against the person, which, by depriving him of his faculties, tries to rob him of his dignity and
to turn him into an object, not of respect, but of pity.

Suffering exposes our *vulnerability*. A chance circumstance,
a small accident of space or time, a small disorder in prenatal
life—all can change the course of a lifetime; can ruin or take
away life. We live from moment to moment at the mercy of
the elements, of a precarious biochemical balance within our
own bodies, of the uneven justice of a world filled with wanton
violence, and nowadays at the mercy of a nuclear event that
could happen at any moment, not merely because of the vola-
tility of politics, but because of an error in a computer chip.

Suffering—passivity, violability, vulnerability—has a transcendental sense. It provides a kind of locus in which an abyss
opens up, in which the familiar categories of everydayness are
shattered. Suffering is one of those surfaces—the face, the sur-
face, of the sufferer—which harbors and shelters within itself
an abyss. The self as abyss. The face as the sur-face over an
abyss. For suffering is not simply suffering. It is a phenomenon
of such proportion that it surpasses itself. An abyss opens up

within it and we find ourselves exposed to the depths, to the mystery, to the desert within us all. Something, who knows what, is at work here—where the body is degraded and reduced to a shadow of its true powers. Suffering is not understandable. It is a violence with no rights, yet it breaks into and ravages our lives.

I treat suffering as a kind of place, a locus, a field in which a radical hermeneutic event takes place, a deep interpretive construal of our existence. In suffering we encounter a darkness which we construe in conflicting ways and with a conflict that cannot be resolved. The ambiguity here is inextinguishable, the interpretations are in conflict, the choices we make uncertain. We come here to that fine part of the soul, that deep ground which Eckhart described, the desert within. It is in this desert that the fundamental lines of our relationship to the world are drawn. Here, in this desert, we wrestle with the powers of darkness, with the angel of death.

For the religious spirit, suffering points to a power which *must* take the side of the sufferer. It is an outrage that cries out for justice. The stars cannot follow their regular course, nor the seasons their sequence, there can be no order or sense in anything, if suffering goes unanswered, if no deeper power intervenes by directing it to some purpose. The most powerful religious image in the Western world—the image of the Cross—is of one who suffers. The central image of Christianity is of a suffering innocent. The image of Jesus, J. B. Metz says, provokes the "disturbing memory of suffering."[10]

Suffering compels us to think that there is a God and that He stands with the sufferer, with the poor and oppressed, the starving and the downtrodden. This deep-set religious view cuts across the ideologies of left and right. That is why liberation theology flourishes in Central America and Catholic priests and nuns are called Marxists because they stand by the poor, while in Poland, where the priests also stand with the poor, with the people, with those who have no voice, they are called counter-revolutionary. Suffering and oppression have a transcendent, a surpassing quality for us. There is more to suffering than lies on its surface. Suffering is not simply suffering, not merely a surface. The face of one who suffers is an arrow, an indication, a clue that God stands on the side of suffering. For the religious spirit, the cries of those who suffer issue from the separation of the soul from God—in keeping with the sentiment of St. Augustine (perhaps the most religious writer the West has produced): "Thou hast made us for thyself, O Lord, and our hearts will not rest until they rest in Thee."

Yet it is precisely suffering that, for Nietzsche, breeds the fiction of religion, the illusion which we call faith. Religion, he says, is devised precisely *"for sufferers*; they maintain that all those who suffer from life as from an illness are in the right, and would like every other feeling of life to be counted false and become impossible. . . ." In the place of the religious response to suffering, Nietzsche puts what he calls an Olympian, Dionysian *laughter*. Such a laughter—the laughter of the young shepherd who bit off the head of the serpent, the laughter for which Zarathustra longs—has taken its full measure of human suffering. It has seen into the abyss of the going-under, has undergone the tragic, suffered from terrible melancholy and nausea, yet nonetheless it affirms this world with all its tragic flaws, affirms the flux of going-over and going-under, and is willing to live without appeal. The ability of a spirit to suffer, Nietzsche says, *almost* determines its nobility. Almost: because it requires likewise the power of laughter.[11]

I do not seek a way to adjudicate this ambiguity and undecidability. I want rather to let this ambiguous and undecidable substructure of our lives be seen, precisely as the nourishing matrix of our beliefs—whether they are religious or tragic, holy or unholy, whether we follow Augustine or Nietzsche. The essential thing is the transcendence, the surpassing, the abyss that opens up under our hands.

My aim is not to produce either an apologia for religion or a critique of it, but to point to the deep ground in which all such fundamental decisions are made, where all essential projects are formed.[12] I want only to mark off the place within us which I have called here mystery, ambiguity, undecidability, the desert, and which lies at the far remove of proof and disproof, of scientific determination. The ambiguity does not dissolve, even though we make a decision, what I would call a deep decision, a deep hermeneutic resolve, a deep construal. I do not want to resolve the ambiguity, or to recommend a course of action, but to point to an ontological structure, to evoke a sense of the hidden depths, of the fine point of the soul, the point where we are brought up short, solicited, shaken, provoked.

Indeed, were one to recommend that we should ignore such numinous considerations altogether and, like Rorty, say that the only point is to minimize suffering and maximize cooperation and to stop dawdling over misty depths, I would not have a counter-argument—except to ask whether anything essential lies outside the sphere of argument. If someone were to say to me that he simply was not interested in this sphere which I want to evoke, I can think of nothing more to say to him.

I am concerned, then, not with an *apologia* for the religious (or the irreligious), nor with its *critique*, but with its *genesis*, its point of departure in the pre-conceptual base of our existence, which I take to be like a dark, thick, ambiguous cord that ties us to the world. I want only to point to the depths and to the ways in which we construe them. Here, in this place, essential decisions are made, fundamental projects are shaped by experiences that go all the way down, experiences that cut all the way through to the core. Heidegger's spatial metaphor of the *da*, the place where something essential happens, serves us well here.

CONCLUSION

The person, then, on my accounting, is a certain play between the sur-face and the abyss. The person is an interplay between two elements. On the one hand, the person is an incarnate project (I take the face to be but the center in which our bodily project as a whole is concentrated) that is intimately interwoven with the world and absorbed in worldly affairs; on the other hand, a power of transcendence which cannot be saturated by any mundane or quotidian operation, which keeps breaking through everydayness, surpassing it, and opening out on to the abyss. The person is the place where that happens, the locus of the transcendence. The resonance we detect in the *per-sona* is the rumbling of this transcendence.

It is as if we cannot be taken in by the world, as if there is more to us than particular worldly engagements can offer. Things have for us a surpassing quality. They serve as occasions of transcendence, which prevents them from retaining their own identity. The simplest things can become occasions of transcendence and hence can become deep. The deepest, most important things are definable by their lack of identity with themselves. Suffering is not merely suffering: it speaks of eternal things—and let us not forget that this does not necessarily mean a religious eternity, but perhaps the eternity of eternal recurrence, the eternity of the infinite flux of the world. The person is a power of converting the finite into the infinite. Let us not say convert, let us say rather breaking through, the place where the infinite breaks through the finite. It is as if we walk on a surface that is constantly ready to give way and to drop us into the abyss. It is as if the world is constantly liable to transmute, to metamorphose, into eternal things. It is as if we lead lives of everyday activity that are always on the edge of breaking through into the extraordinary, the abnormal, the exceptional. One imagines life as a kind of surrealist film in which a man walking down a crowded city street turns a corner only to find himself in a desert, alone with himself, thinking eternal thoughts. It is as if there is a hidden hair-trigger in things which can be set off by the slightest gesture, the smallest movement, yet produce a shattering blow, a shocking force that leaves us shaken.

Our lives are lived out in this interplay between these two spheres. But this is no theory of two worlds, of inner soul and outer world, eternity and time. Rather, the things of our world have two dimensions, two sides: on the one side their identity—the face of one who suffers is a face and nothing more—and on the other side their non-identity, their power of eliciting surpassal and transcendence, their power to spin off into infinity. And let us say that the person is the being in whom these two, identity and surpassal, intersect. The person is the place where things open up, where the infinity harbored within them is exposed, where the abyss breaks open, where the desert encroaches.

In the person there is played out an interplay between sur-face and depth, ordinary and extraordinary, commonplace and mystery. The Being of the person is to be open to this inter-play, to be the place where transcendence occurs, to let the mystery of Being, of the withdrawal of Being, come to pass. The person is the locus where the transformation of the com-monplace into the abyss occurs. And everything that we mean by religion and art and philosophy is, it seems to me, an at-tempt to come to grips with this transformation, to let it happen, to preserve and cultivate it with words.

Per-sona: the old word for sounding-through. *Per-sona*: the abyss sounding through the sur-face, the sur-face that keeps opening up on to the abyss. *Per-sona*: the concealment that inhabits the core of, and resonates in, all un-concealment. *Per-sona*: the sounding of the mystery, of the withdrawal of Being, the echo it leaves behind.

Whose voice is sounding through the person? Is it the voice of God calling us down the labyrinthine way? Or is it no voice at all, but simply the rumble of the world-play, of the flux, and the more-than-human laughter of Zarathustra, danc-ing and singing even as he goes under?

NOTES

1. Heidegger too seems willing to give the old word *per-sona* a second reading. He writes: "*Persona* means the actor's mask through which his dramatic tale is sounded. Since man is the percipient who perceives what is, we can think of him as the *persona*, the mask, of Being" (*What is Called Thinking?*, trans. F. Wieck and J. Glenn Gray [New York: Harper & Row, 1968], p. 62). The project

of a phenomenology of the face has been initiated by Emmanuel Levinas, most notably in his *Totality and Infinity*, trans. A. Lingis (Pittsburgh: Duquesne University Press, 1969). See the writings of Robert Bernasconi and Adrian Peperzak for suggestive attempts to relate the work of Heidegger and Levinas.

2. See in particular "Action as the Self-Revelation of Being: A Central Theme in the Thought of St. Thomas," in *History of Philosophy in the Making*, ed. Linus Thro (Washington: University Press of America, 1982), pp. 63–80; "Interpersonal Dialogue: Key to Realism," in *Person and Community*, ed. Robert J. Roth, s.j. (New York: Fordham University Press, 1975), pp. 141–53; "The Self in Eastern and Western Thought: The Wooster Conference," *International Philosophical Quarterly*, 6 (1969), 101–109; "The Self as the Source of Meaning in Metaphysics," *Review of Metaphysics*, 21 (1968), 587–614.

3. "Action as the Self-Revelation of Being," p. 71.

4. See my "Kant's Ethics in Phenomenological Perspective," in *Kant and Phenomenology*, ed. Thomas Seebohm (Washington: University Press of America, 1984), pp. 129–46.

5. Martin Heidegger, *The Basic Problems of Phenomenology*, trans. A. Hofstadter (Bloomington: Indiana University Press, 1984), pp. 132–37.

6. In the *First Logical Investigation*, § 5, Husserl argues that gestures are merely indicative, not meaningful, signs.

7. It is in this way that, following the recent work of William Richardson, one can integrate the Heideggerian problematic with the question of the unconscious. See "Lacan and the Subject of Psychoanalysis," in *Psychiatry and the Humanities*, Vol. 6. *Interpreting Lacan*, edd. J. Smith and W. Kerrigan (New Haven: Yale University Press, 1983), pp. 51–74.

8. See Levinas' discussion of ethics and the face in *Infinity and Totality*, Part Two, pp. 194–219.

9. I take this critique of value from Heidegger; see in particular *Der Satz vom Grund* (Pfullingen: Neske, 1957), pp. 34–35. To a great extent Heidegger's critique of ethics is a critique of modern or metaphysical ethics.

10. Johann Baptist Metz, *Faith in History and Society: Toward a Practical Fundamental Theology*, trans. D. Smith (New York: Crossroad/Seabury, 1980), pp. 88–118. See also Matthew Lamb, *Solidarity with Victims* (New York: Crossroad, 1982).

11. Nietzsche, *Beyond Good and Evil*, trans. R. J. Hollingdale (New York: Penguin, 1973). Compare aphorisms #62, #270, and #294.

12. Father Clarke addresses this same issue in his discussion of Transcendental Thomism in *The Philosophical Approach to God: A Neo-Thomist Perspective* (Winston-Salem: Wake Forest University, 1979), sect. I, esp. pp. 21–22.

Process and Thomist Views Concerning Divine Perfection

Lewis S. Ford

Old Dominion University

FORTY YEARS AGO, Charles Hartshorne launched a pointed polemic against the Thomistic contention that God is not really related to the world.[1] For a long time this challenge was virtually ignored, but in 1973 W. Norris Clarke, S.J. inaugurated an important conversation between Thomistic and process philosophies in his rejoinder on "A New Look at the Immutability of God."[2]

Clarke's argument uses the distinction between God's real being, which is clearly regarded as immutable, and God's intentionality. Now, an actuality has intentional being insofar as it is an object of knowledge or love existing in the consciousness of another. As such "it has no real being of its own, but exists entirely within the consciousness of the knower, with an 'existence' or presence given and maintained entirely by the real act of knowing in the knower."[3] This intentional mode of being is required for any act of knowledge whenever what is known differs in real being from the knower itself, and hence applies to God's knowledge of a world distinct from himself.

Now, God's intentional field of consciousness, containing all the intentional objects of his knowledge and love, necessarily includes all his creatures in their individuality, and this field would have been contingently other than what it is if God had created a different world from this. Through his intentional consciousness God is *truly* related to us whom he has freely created, even though he is not *really* related to us in the technical sense, which would require God to be affected in his intrinsic real being by the relation. The fact that the intentional contents of God's consciousness are multiple and contingent does not require, Clarke claims, that God's intrinsic being likewise is. Nonetheless this is an authentic personal relation in God to us, so that he is truly other and different in his consciousness because of his relations to us. Thus the essential demand of religious sensibility is met: we do make a difference to God.[4]

Moreover, Clarke suggests a way God can know our free actions without either determining them or being acted upon by them and thereby be changed. Let us suppose that God freely offers his indeterminate abundance of power to us, allowing us to channel and determine its flow. Then the determination we contribute does not add any new being to the divine power, but simply delimits its plenitude. "So God can know my free action by knowing just how I allow His freely offered power, always gently drawing me through the good, to flow through me. He knows my choice by knowing His own active power working within me, as thus determined or channeled determinately here and now by me."[5] Basic to this argument is the acute insight that "the crucial moment in free decision is *not a doing at all*. It is precisely the moment of *negation* or *exclusion* of all possible avenues of choice save one. . . ."[6] The positive act upon which our free determination then depends is God's creative act in us, and it is by means of this that he knows our free actions.[7]

With further reflection, in the course of discussing the extent to which process philosophy might be compatible with Thomistic theism, Clarke is prepared to concede "that God can be said in some significant though carefully qualified way to be both (1) *really related* to the world in His intentional consciousness and (2) contingently *different*, even *mutable* (though not necessarily so, since the 'eternal Now' view of God is still viable), *because of* what happens in the created world (hence truly affected, enriched by new modalities of joy due to our responses)—but all this only in His relational, intentional consciousness."[8]

If we emphasize all the careful qualifications, I suppose that it is possible to construe this as a merely rhetorical shift on Clarke's part. But I take it to be a very important shift in light of the fact that Clarke had already worked out the logic of how God is *not* really related to the world more adequately than any other thinker in confronting the process challenge. Moreover, this shift follows naturally from Clarke's earlier appreciation of what perfect knowledge entails: "For it cannot be an imperfection to know what is not in itself knowable—i.e., the future, the not yet real, at least in its free or not yet determined aspects. Perfect knowledge of an evolving reality would by nature have to evolve with its object."[9]

Now, in a recent critique, Theodore J. Kondoleon argues that "This last statement is made gratuitously and is obviously false. Perfect knowledge, even of an evolving object, cannot evolve without itself being imperfect. . . ."[10] Yet is it *obviously* false? Clarke did not think so. Two different notions of perfect knowing seem to be operative here. Clarke is thinking of what knowing might be, if that knowing were perfectly contoured to its object, even if emergent, while Kondoleon considers rather the knowledge that a perfect being might have, assuming that being to be absolutely immutable. Such immutable knowledge may be what is appropriate to a perfect being, but it throws into jeopardy the possibility of any knowing perfectly contoured to its object, if there is any genuine emergence. Which is perfect knowing: that which is perfectly apportioned to its object, or the knowing that a perfect being must have?

A powerful assumption underlying Kondoleon's entire essay is the identification of knowledge and being in divine simplicity, such that any change in divine knowledge necessarily undercuts the immutability of perfect being. Clarke can be successful only so far as this identification can be mitigated.

Even Kondoleon, however, cannot avoid *some* distinction between divine knowledge and divine immutability. In addressing the question whether God's knowledge *could* have been different had there not been a world, he notes that God

> would be the same infinite or perfect being without it. Yet on the supposition that God wills to create, then He must possess such knowledge. Such knowledge, then, may be said to be completely unnecessary to God (as creatures are), i.e., something not required by the divine perfection but nonetheless something it could not be without on the supposition that God wills to create. . . . Hence such knowledge in no way implies an addition to the divine being, perfection, or understanding or any change in God's being or understanding (which are always and necessarily one and the same).[11]

Nevertheless God's knowledge would be different if the world were to exist rather than not. God's knowledge of his own creative power would differ. Kondoleon's arguments merely show that such knowledge would make no difference to God's immutable *being*. If we must (implicitly) distinguish here between God's mutable knowledge and his immutable being, perhaps Clarke can make the distinction elsewhere. From a process perspective, however, this mutable knowledge is still quite unsatisfactory, since any knowledge must be utterly worthless that cannot enrich the divine being in any way.

God's intentional consciousness is really related to the contingent world, Clarke tells us, but how is God's intentional consciousness and his own inner being related? God's own inner being cannot be really related to the divine intentional consciousness without denying its perfect immutability. Yet nothing divine can be merely externally related to God's inner being without jeopardizing pure simplicity. Clarke sometimes speaks of the intentional consciousness as nothing with respect to the perfection of God's inner being, but this may confuse intentional consciousness with the being of objects of consciousness. To be sure, an object of knowledge "has no real being of its own, but exists entirely within the consciousness of the knower,"[12] but does this apply to the consciousness itself? Subjective existence is not the same as objective existence. Objective existence is merely derivative, depending upon the independent existence of the subject entertaining the object. But we have seen that any subject must be really related to a contingent object in order for the object to have intentional being. Were it unaffected by the object, such intentional existence would have no grounding. Intentional consciousness would not even have the status of intentional being if it cannot be really related to God's inner being.

Let us reverse the poles of this relationship, and inquire whether God's intentional consciousness could be really related to his inner being. If the immutable cannot include the mutable, perhaps the mutable could include the immutable. Charles Hartshorne, in a seminal article, posed just this question.[13] Given a totality that is both dynamic and static, what would the whole be? It could not be static, for if it changed in any part, then the whole would be changed to that extent. Only the dynamic could be the more inclusive. If there is also divine intentional consciousness, it would include any immutable inner being. For the intentional consciousness is contingent upon a changing, temporal world, and is therefore dynamic. From a Hartshornean perspective, the intentional consciousness is also necessarily dynamic simply because it is subjective. As subject it includes all intentional being as its object, as well as God's inner being. In fact, if we make God's intentional consciousness ontologically the more fundamental, even God's inner being takes on the purely derivative status of intentional being.

This is precisely what happens in Hartshorne's theism and in the Hartshornean interpretation of Whitehead's God: the timeless, immutable 'primordial nature' acquires a purely objective status.[14] For Hartshorne, it is merely abstract, which is included within God's concrete, temporal experience.

Whether or not the primordial nature alone has an abstract or an intentional being, it is understood by Whitehead to be continually enriched by God's consequent experience of the world. It cannot simply be identified with the fullness of God as existing alone prior to, or apart from, the creation of the world. If God already possesses all the riches of perfection beforehand, temporal existence can add nothing. Nothing of all we experience firsthand, or know ourselves to be, can contribute to that divine life, and hence is deprived of any ultimate significance.

Yet it is clear that the primordial nature, while immutable since non-temporal, cannot itself be perfect if God seeks enrichment from the world. This is the deepest sense in which Whitehead's God is thought to be finite. I have tried to show all the ways in which this conception is truly infinite,[15] but as long as it is capable of enrichment in any sense, it is deemed finite. I do not think it is so much finite as imperfect, imperfect in the sense that it is not all-inclusive: something yet remains outside its unity. Hartshorne's emendation, whereby God is conceived to be a continuing series of divine beings, each surpassing its predecessors and unsurpassed by any other actualities, can also be considered as finite, since every divine being, itself capable of being surpassed by some future divine being, must therefore be finite.

But then, for Whitehead, *all* being, if determinate, must be finite. For something to be determinately existent, it must be *this* rather than *that*: "all actualization is finite [and] involves the exclusion of alternative possibility."[16] This is precisely what distinguishes actual being from the infinitude of possibility.

We seem to have reached an impasse. In order to be perfect, God would seem to be necessarily immutable, but such immutability wars against such important features as the divine subjectivity and intentional consciousness, particularly any awareness of the contingent, temporal world. These are also perfections. How are we to understand the perfection of God in the light of such difficulties?

Let us first examine the reasons why immutability is thought to be necessary for divine perfection. If God is pure being, and being is strictly convertible with unity, then God must be the supreme instance of unity. The unity that God has must be the most intense form of unity possible, a unity beyond the unity of mere composition. Hence God must be perfectly simple, with no really distinguishable parts.

If God has no parts, God can have no temporal contrasts within himself. 'Before' and 'after' cannot be distinguished, and any change would be impossible. For this to be the case, God would have to be timeless, rather than, as in Scripture, everlasting, lasting throughout all time, the one who was, and is, and is to come. Besides, any change which a perfect being could undergo could be only for the worse.[17]

Notice that this reasoning is purely *a priori*. God's necessary attributes, except for knowledge (assuming, for the moment, that God necessarily knows that which is contingent), remains precisely the same whether the world exists or not. Even that knowledge is immutably the same (from a timeless perspective, to be sure) whether God dwells in solitary splendor before the world began, or with the world (assuming, for the moment, that it is meaningful for the world to have a finite temporal beginning). No matter how we experience, or conceive, reality to be, God's nature remains the same.

The logic of divine perfection is totally independent of human experience, and thus is a classic candidate for Kant's opprobrium, "dogmatic metaphysics." Kant's own stricture that all non-dogmatic metaphysics must be restricted to the conditions for any possible experience should not blind us to the breadth of his critique. For Kant, metaphysics should be explanatory of what we actually experience. Now, dogmatic metaphysics might explain our world, but only in a merely accidental fashion, for nothing requires it to be adequate or applicable to our experience. There is nothing in an *a priori* approach that necessarily ties it to experience. If the initial principles are truly self-evident, and the deductions correct, then so much the worse for reality as ordinarily experienced.

Although Whitehead refers to his own philosophy as "a recurrence to pre-Kantian modes of thought,"[18] it is definitely not a return to pre-critical metaphysics. The absolute certainty of self-evident first principles is replaced by tentative hypotheses. The same methods of imaginative generalization and deduction are retained, but these deductions are then compared with our experience to determine their adequacy and applicability.[19] If it cannot explain our experience, then the first principles need to be revised. They are not *a priori* as independent of experience, but spring from experience as their final basis.

Were dogmatic metaphysics appropriate, there would be nothing wrong with the divine perfection of being. But the demands of our experience are insistent, so that we need to account for contingency and the divine relation to contingency. This theme encompasses a number of topics, classically the question of God's knowledge of future contingents,[20] but also such issues as God's involvement with our particular temporal affairs, intercessory prayer as making a difference to God, and divine suffering for the contingent evils of the world. If God reconciles the world to himself through Christ's taking upon himself the sins of the world, it seems strange to those not grasped by the logic of divine immutability that God should be immune to all suffering in the experience of evil.

Yet what is the theist to do? He must believe that God exists, and that God is perfect. A perfect being is necessarily immutable. This the process theist must grant the Thomist. Any divine being that changes is imperfect, and can be considered to be finite. But if so, how can we deal satisfactorily with the contingent with respect to God?

While the theist must believe God to be perfect, it is not necessarily to think that God is being. As we have seen, Clarke stresses the subjectivity and intentional consciousness of God, features which generally are ascribed to becoming in Whitehead. Whitehead conceived of God as a primordial concrescence, which because timeless is usually considered to be objective being, to which subjective becoming as an everlasting consequent experience of the temporal world was superadded. Yet if we modify this concept solely in terms of pure becoming, then we could understand God to be the perfect instance of becoming.

Then God would be simply everlasting concrescence, that is, the growing together of all things, whether necessary or contingent, within one divine experience. Just as divine being was classically conceived as the perfection of unity, divine becoming is the perfection of unification, drawing all things into greater and greater unity, but continually making room for new contingencies. In place of the static simplicity of immutability, we now have the dynamic simplicity of unification. Because this notion of God is open to contingency, divine perfection when applied to becoming can explain rather than disregard experience. The perfect knower, if perfect becoming, can know emergence in a way perfectly apportioned to it. In this way our two kinds of "perfect knowing" are simply the subjective and objective aspects of the same knowing, not conflicting as they would be if applied to perfect immutable being.

Obj. 1: Yet is not becoming inferior to being as derivative from it?—Here we raise a very large issue beyond the scope of this essay. Suffice it to say that Whitehead's whole endeavor, through a reconception of what is involved in creation, is to show how being is ontologically grounded in becoming, and not the other way around.

Obj. 2: Does not this render the world necessary, for finite beings are continually needed as material for the divine unifying experience?—Yes, but then the whole distinction between necessary and contingent being needs revision. If we adopt perfect becoming as our model of God, then God can no longer be considered to be wholly necessary. God would have both necessary and contingent aspects. Yet such would also be true of all actualities. To be sure, the necessary features of finite actualities may not be very many (e.g., occupy space-time, be the outcome of past causation, etc.), but they are nonetheless quite real. If this is the case, there would not be one transcendent act whereby God wills that there be a world or not, but God still largely determines what kind of a world exists in any cosmic epoch. Instead of there being one single transcendent creative act, creation is pluralized into many immanent instances of temporal self-creation guided by divine initiatives.[21]

Obj. 3: Yet if God is solely becoming, never achieving being, then God never becomes anything.—If God is now only in a state of becoming, Wolfhart Pannenberg recognizes that it would be "necessary to say that, in a restricted but important sense, God does not yet exist. . . . God's being is still in the process of coming to be. Considering this, God should not be mistaken for an objectified being presently existing in its fullness."[22]

Yet Pannenberg conceives God finally to come into being at the end of time, at the culmination of history. Process theism considers the future to be absolutely open-ended, for the cessation of the beings of the world, were it possible, would also mean the termination of God's existence as becoming. God never becomes a being, to be sure, but this is no serious objection unless we were to conceive God to be an independent actuality. Paul Tillich has insisted that God could not be such a being.[23] Rather than being a being, God is a factor in the creation of the finite beings of the world. All beings, as determinately *this* rather than *that*, are finite, but they could not come into being apart from God. These finite beings, moreover, find their ultimate significance in the everlasting unification of the divine becoming. Becoming is not being, but it is a necessary factor for all being.

Despite this basic contrast between perfect being and perfect becoming, the conversation between Thomistic and process philosophies has shown a profound and striking convergence: Whiteheadian creativity is the process counterpart to Thomstic *esse*. In both philosophies it is the ontological foundation of all actualities. If Whitehead's philosophy is modified by reconceiving God as pure becoming, as ultimate creativity, as here advocated, it is possible to see God as the source of creativity underlying all finite beings.[24] This surely is in line with the Thomistic vision.

The difference lies in Thomas' presupposition of a substantialist ontology, which allows divinely created beings to exercise then their own freedom. In Whitehead's event ontology, the creation and the activity of an event are one and the same. Hence if God were to create the event, that being could have no freedom of self-determination. For Thomas, God creates the being by communicating to it its act of being. In my modification of Whitehead, God communicates to the creature its power of becoming whereby the creature acts by creating itself. In Thomas the perfection of the infinite act of being lies in its simplicity and immutability, whereas for Whitehead the perfection of the source of becoming may be found in an everlasting concrescence including within itself all temporal, contingent being.

NOTES

1. *The Divine Relativity: A Social Conception of God* (New Haven: Yale University Press, 1948).

2. In *God Knowable and Unknowable*, ed. Robert J. Roth, s.j. (New York: Fordham University Press, 1973), pp. 43–72. For my appreciation of and response to this essay, see "The Immutable God and Father Clarke," *The New Scholasticism*, 49 No. 2 (Spring 1975), 189–99.

Since the publication of Clarke's essay, a number of papers have been published contributing to some aspect of the process/Thomist discussion. Besides those mentioned later in this essay, they include:

Bracken, Joseph A., s.j. *The Triune Symbol: Persons, Process and Community*. College Theology Society, Studies in Religion, 1. Lanham, Md.: University Press of America, 1985.

Burrell, David B., c.s.c. "Does Process Theology Rest on a Mistake?," *Theological Studies*, 43 No. 1 (March 1982), 125–35.

Devenish, Philip E. "Postliberal Process Theology: A Rejoinder to Burrell," *Theological Studies*, 43 (1982), 504–13.

Galot, J., s.j. "La Realité de la souffrance de Dieu," *Nouvelle Revue Théologique*, 101 (March 1979), 224–45.

Hallman, Joseph M. "The Necessity of the World in Thomas Aquinas and Alfred North Whitehead," *The Modern Schoolman*, 40 No. 4 (May 1983), 264–72.

Hill, William, O.P. "Does the World Make a Difference to God?,"
The Thomist, 38 No. 1 (January 1974), 146–64.

———. "Does God Know the Future? Aquinas and Some Moderns,"
Theological Studies, 36 No. 1 (March 1975), 3–18.

———. "Two Gods of Love: Aquinas and Whitehead," *Listening*,
14 (1976), 249–64.

Kelly, Anthony J. "God: How Near a Relation?," *The Thomist*, 34
(1970), 191–229.

Trethowan, Iltyd. *Process Theology and the Christian Tradition*.
Still River, Mass.: St. Bede's Publications, 1985.

Whitney, Barry. "Divine Immutability in Process Philosophy and
Contemporary Thomism," *Horizons*, 7 (1980), 49–68.

Wright, John H., S.J. "Divine Knowledge and Human Freedom:
The God Who Dialogues," *Theological Studies*, 38 No. 3 (September 1977), 450–77.

———. "The Method of Process Theology: An Evaluation," *Communio*, 6 No. 1 (Spring 1979), 38–55.

In addition, an entire issue of *The Modern Schoolman* (62 No. 4
[May 1985]) is devoted to papers presented at a conference on Process Philosophy and Theology held at Saint Louis University in
March 1985 by Charles Hartshorne, Leonard J. Eslick, David
Tracy, Lewis S. Ford, Theodore R. Vitali, C.P., Thomas E. Hosinski, C.S.C., Daniel Dombrowski, and Thomas J. Regan, S.J.

Though not with respect to the immutabilist response to the
Hartshornean challenge, there was the anticipation of a *rapprochement* between process and Thomist themes in the writings of the
late Walter Stokes, S.J., such as his "A Whiteheadian Reflection
on God's Relation to the World," in *Process Theology*, ed. Ewert
Cousins (New York: Newman Press, 1971), pp. 137–52; "God
for Today and Tomorrow," in *Process Philosophy and Christian
Thought*, edd. Brown, James, and Reeves (Indianapolis: Bobbs–
Merrill, 1971), pp. 244–63; "Is God Really Related to This
World?," *Proceedings of the American Catholic Philosophical Association*, 39 (1965), 145–51; and "Freedom as a Perfection: Whitehead, Thomas, and Augustine," ibid., 36 (1962), 134–42.

3. Clarke, "A New Look," p. 53.
4. Ibid., pp. 56ff.
5. Ibid., p. 68.
6. Ibid., p. 69; italics his.

7. For my examination and response to this argument, see "The Immutable God and Father Clarke," 189–99.

8. "Christian Theism and Whiteheadian Process Philosophy: Are They Compatible?," in W. Norris Clarke, s.j., *The Philosophical Approach to God* (Winston-Salem: Wake Forest University, 1979), pp. 66–109 at p. 102. (For a rejoinder to this essay on one specific topic—affirming the need for some source for Whiteheadian creativity, but questioning whether it can be found in the efficient causality of the past—see my "The Search for the Source of Creativity," *Logos*, 1 [1980], 45–52.)

9. Clarke, "A New Look," p. 65.

10. "The Immutability of God: Some Recent Challenges," *The New Scholasticism*, 58 No. 3 (Summer 1983), 293–315, at 303.

11. Kondoleon, pp. 311f.

12. Clarke, "A New Look," p. 53, quoted above, at n. 3.

13. "Process as Inclusive Category: A Reply," *The Journal of Philosophy*, 52 No. 4 (February 17, 1955), 94–102.

14. Whitehead, however, always insisted on the existence of a non-temporal divine subjectivity, even though now combined with a temporal divine subjectivity as well: see my essay on "The Non-Temporality of Whitehead's God," *International Philosophical Quarterly*, 13 No. 3 (September 1973), 347–76. I now find this notion of a timeless subjectivity quite problematic.

15. "The Infinite God of Process Theism," *Proceedings of the American Catholic Philosophical Association*, 55 (1981), 84–90.

16. Alfred North Whitehead, *Adventures of Ideas* (New York: Macmillan, 1933), p. 333.

17. This is intended as a general argument, undergirding much of traditional theism. It does not follow Aquinas' explicit argumentation, which seeks to be as *a posteriori* as possible. His primary argument for immutability seems to require reasoning from motion to an unmoved mover. Insofar as the argument is kept strictly empirical, and is not metaphysicized by generalizing 'motus' to apply to any activity whatsoever, it is inextricably bound up with the Aristotelian physics of motion, now superseded by Newton's principle of inertial motion. Yet, whatever the fate of these *a posteriori* arguments, divine immutability continues to be insisted upon. Some sort of *a priori* argument, based on the logic of divine perfection, seems to be at work here.

18. *Process and Reality* (New York: Macmillan, 1929), p. vi.

19. Ibid., p. 4.

20. In general, this essay presupposes the process critique of Thomas' conception of the divine knowledge of future contingents, classically developed by Charles Hartshorne in *The Divine Relativity*. For an even-handed presentation of both sides, see John C. Moskop, *Divine Omniscience and Human Freedom: Thomas Aquinas and Charles Hartshorne* (Macon: Mercer University Press, 1984). John F. Wippel carefully expounds Aquinas' position in his contribution to *Divine Omniscience and Omnipotence in Medieval Philosophy*, ed. T. Rudavsky (Dordrecht: Reidel, 1985).

As I understand it, Thomas regards God's knowledge of future contingents to be immutable because knowledge must accord with the being of the knower, which in this case is eternal. Moreover, God creates whatever is divinely known.

That knowledge must accord with the being of the knower seems to be a sound principle. There are surely differences between the way an insentient bar of iron receives heat, the sensations a clam receives, and the intelligent perceptions alert human beings can have. Here the mode of being differs, and it makes a decided difference. For example, there must be conscious attention, absent from a bar of iron, for the perception of color. At the same time, this principle seems quite one-sided. Perception *also* depends upon the character of what is perceived, at least in all instances empirically known to us. Attention alone cannot tell us whether what we are attending to is red or green.

The basic reason for not extending this second principle to the divine experience is derived from the logic of divine perfection, assuming that receptivity would require passive potentiality in God. This need not be the case. As I have argued elsewhere, receptivity is essential for the activity of unification, and is more properly understood as active rather than passive: "Whitehead's Transformation of Pure Act," *The Thomist*, 41 No. 3 (July 1977), 381–99.

If God were devoid of any receptive capacity, there would be no difference between perception and imagination in the divine experience. Perhaps this is felt to be no problem if God knows by creating. Yet, if God only knows what God creates, then either God creates evil or evil cannot be divinely known. The same reasoning applies equally well to creaturely freedom. God can know our freedom only insofar as it is divinely created, not insofar as we have made use of it, except perhaps in the fashion Father Clarke has outlined for it.

Immutable knowledge excludes all novelty and adventure from the divine experience. Are not these perfections worthy of the divine?

The problem with divine knowledge of future contingents is even more of a problem for the contingent events themselves. Are they *now* determinate? If not, then it is false to "know" them as determinate, no matter from what perspective. If so, then our actions cannot determine them otherwise, so the temporality and freedom we experience must be fundamentally illusory.

21. Here see my essay "An Alternative to *Creatio ex nihilo*," *Religious Studies*, 19 No. 2 (June 1983), 205–13.

22. *Theology and the Kingdom of God* (Philadelphia: Westminster Press, 1969), p. 56.

23. See, e.g., *Systematic Theology*, I (Chicago: University of Chicago Press, 1951), 235f.

24. Here see my essays on "The Divine Activity of the Future," *Process Studies*, 11 No. 3 (Fall 1981), 169–79, and "Creativity in a Future Key," in *New Essays in Metaphysics*, ed. Robert C. Neville (Albany: State University of New York Press, 1986).

The Two Journeys
to the Divine Presence

JOHN E. SMITH

Yale University

EVERY STUDENT OF THE HISTORY of Western philosophy and
theology is familiar with the two great religious traditions
that developed as the result of efforts to determine the proper
relations between the two ultimates, Being and God, and their
articulation in reason and faith. These traditions, the ontological and the cosmological, representing two distinct *ways*
or *journeys* to God, are familiarly identified as the ontological
and cosmological *arguments* for the existence of God. In one
sense this identification is unfortunate, not only because it
obscures the fact that the ontological *way* of ascent to God had
received brilliant expression at the hands of Augustine centuries before it was cast in the form of *the* ontological argument by Anselm, but also because emphasis on neatly pack-
aged arguments fails to do justice to the richness and the
profundity of the two types of *religious apprehension* underlying the respective traditions. For these reasons, I find it more
appropriate to view them as two journeys or ways to God, each
with its own assumptions, method, and culmination.

I see the form of spirituality characteristic of Augustine,
Anselm, Bonaventure, and Alexander of Hales that is rooted
in self-knowledge and meditative thinking, and the form of
spirituality represented by Thomas Aquinas and Albertus
Magnus that sets out from the world and natural existence
together with a firm belief in the power of demonstrative reason, *as ways of making explicit* two different patterns of *intel-*

ligibility in religion. I use the term "intelligibility" here purposely because I should like to avoid the term "proof," since that term is more appropriate for abstract and formal disciplines such as mathematics and logic than for studies as concrete as philosophical theology. I seriously doubt whether it is legitimate to speak of any large-scale thesis concerning what there is as capable of proof in the sense, for example, in which it is legitimate to speak of proving the theorem that there is no last prime number. I do not regard this as in any sense an avowal of skepticism, but rather an acknowledgement of the truth expressed in Aristotle's claim that the nature of the subject matter must always be an important factor determining the form of rationality appropriate for understanding it. Speaking of two different patterns of intelligibility makes it possible to avoid an error and at the same time do justice to the important difference between the two traditions in this respect. As for the error, it has often been supposed that the Augustinian way is all *immediate* or *intuitive* and the Thomist way is all *inferential* and *demonstrative*, and therefore that the latter has the greater claim to logical cogency. That this view misrepresents Augustine's original position is clear, not only from an examination of his doctrinal writings, but from his most illuminating summary account of his procedure in the final book of the *Trinity* as well. "I will attempt," Augustine writes, "by the help of God, to the best of my power, to put briefly together *without arguing*, whatever I have *established in the several books of arguments as known*, and to place, as it were, under one mental view, not the way in which we have been convinced of each point, but the points themselves of which we have been convinced. . . ."[1] This passage shows the presence of argument and processes of thought; the way of ascent is dialectical and not all "immediate" as Tillich seems to think.

There is, however, a difference in the two patterns of intelligibility not to be overlooked: the Augustinian way, brilliantly illustrated later in Bonaventure's *Itinerarium*, is a journey of rational or dialectical ascent to God, and the first principles (*Sapientia*) in terms of which everything is to be understood, whereas the Thomistic way is an inferential journey from a given existence and some of its features better known to us aimed at reaching the divine existence that is not directly available to us apart from the inferential process involving the principle of causality. Despite the difference involved and even the fact that, for a variety of understandable reasons, Thomas dismissed the ontological way, it is still possible to construe each way as expressing a distinct pattern of intelligibility, thus paving the way for a reconsideration of their relations to each other and of the possibility that there may be a unifying link between them not previously acknowledged and developed.

Before proceeding further, I would like to introduce an autobiographical note that has a significant bearing on what I am attempting in this discussion. Several decades ago Paul Tillich wrote a paper dealing with the two traditions under the title, "The Two Types of Philosophy of Religion."[2] It is a brilliant piece whether one agrees with it or not, and I cannot think of any other single paper that made such an impact on me philosophically and theologically, so that I have returned to it ever again in order to decide whether his way of relating the two represents a viable solution to this difficult problem. I cannot, of course, attempt to summarize the paper, but a brief account of the main drift of Tillich's analysis will prove helpful.

By means of a vivid and dramatic figure, Tillich described the ontological way to God as the *overcoming*, through the dialectical recovery of *Esse, Verum, Bonum* in both power and thought, of the *estrangement* of man from God that followed from man's rebellion in the Fall. Man and God have become estranged but not separated, and the tarnished image of God in man can be recovered by the renewal of mind. The cosmological way, by contrast, was described by Tillich as the meeting by man of a *Stranger* who is essentially the God whose necessary existence has been asserted through a set of inferences based on the finitude, dependence, and contingency of the world and several of its characteristics. The first way is through the meditative apprehension of meaning expressed in the formula "faith seeking understanding," while the second uses the principle of causality and the incoherence of the infinite regress as the basis for the demonstrative proof of divine existence. What is implied in the figure, of course, is that the God who is reached through the cosmological argument is a reality not previously known to us and, indeed, as has often been pointed out, Thomas found it necessary to end each of his arguments with such words as "and this we call God" and "by this all understand God." The identity was no doubt intended at the outset, but it first becomes explicit only at the end of the proof.

On the basis of the fundamental distinction between the two ways, Tillich's argument is that the ontological way allows for a basic certainty about God through the recovery of the uncreated light in the mind in the form of what later were known as "transcendentals"—*Verum, Bonum, Esse*—or the *Sapientia* (see Augustine, *De Trin.* XII, 14) representing the understanding of divine things and consequently forming the basis for interpreting the things of the world (*De Trin.* XII, 1). The cosmological way, on the contrary, just because it starts with the world, its existence and generic features, and argues via the principle of causality for divine existence, exchanges the meditative certainty attained by starting with the self for a set of arguments meant to be demonstrative in a purely objective way. It is Tillich's contention, and in this I believe he was right, that the difficulties that have surrounded all attempts to derive an *existent* through a linear proof were foreshadowed by the crucial transformation made by Anselm when, departing from the Augustinian position and adopting the Aristotle of Boethius,[3] he proposed a single proof for God's *existence* and thus centered attention on that essential but now abstracted feature of the divine nature. That transformation of the older tradition set in motion the long discussion that continues to this day concerning whether "existence" is a predicate, and it is not without significance that, in order to distinguish the existence to be attributed to God from that possessed by a star or a stone, some thinkers have suggested the distinction between the existence that is not a predicate and the necessary existence that is. The basic problem stems from singling out existence as an abstract feature to be arrived at by an argument, especially since, as was bound to happen, *existence* came to be construed exclusively in terms of finite and contingent things and God cannot be thought to "exist" in that sense.

The cosmological tradition does not escape involvement with this problem, although it is clear that Thomas thought he had avoided the difficulty by dismissing the ontological argument in terms too familiar to need repeating, and by preparing to begin in a new way, which was to start with what is better known to us, in this case the existence of the world. With this new beginning Thomas thought to resolve two problems with one stroke. On the one hand, it would no longer be necessary for us to appeal to the direct apprehension of the divine nature, which he regarded as the basis of Anselm's proof but which is at the same time unavailable to us, and, on the other, Thomas believed that he could avoid the classical objection to Anselm's proof, which says that existence cannot be derived from "mere ideas," by *starting* with an *existence* that all must acknowledge—the world and its features. The principle involved is clear enough—whatever reality is required for accounting for the existence we have in hand must itself exist and cannot have the status of the merely possible. Unfortunately, the vexing problem of the two existences presents itself once again, as the dialectic of modern empiricism up to Kant makes clear. If you argue from finite existence you can argue only to further finite existence, and without a *saltus* you cannot reach an existence of another kind. I have been calling attention to some difficulties that confront each tradition as a prelude to a proposal for reinterpreting each of them in a way that may help to show why both are needed, and how they may be seen not as the same but as different expressions of the same underlying endeavor—what I am calling the two journeys to the divine *Presence*.

To return for a moment to Tillich's analysis, while I believe that he is basically correct in his account of what has actually happened in and to these traditions, I have always been uneasy about two of his points, which is the reason I am attempting to reassess the entire situation. The first is that he overemphasizes the "immediacy" in the ontological way, and thus opens up a seemingly unbridgeable gap between it and the cosmological way which he describes as wholly "inferential." Secondly, and closely related, is the matter of relating the two ways to each other. Tillich proposes to subordinate the cosmological way to the ontological and, while there is a point to this way of connecting them, there is also a coordination between them which, as it seems to me, he has overlooked. In short, the question that has continued to trouble me is whether there is not some unifying link between them, some underlying unity that does not obscure the obvious differences involved, but rather helps to close the gap between the two ways by showing how each can be aiming to reach the same divine reality. At the risk of beginning at the end, let me propose that there is such a link and that it takes the form of emphasis on the divine *Presence*. In order, however, to present this resolution as a development out of the ways themselves, I shall briefly chart the two journeys—the figure, of course, is borrowed from Bonaventure—paying special attention to their respective starting-points, their distinctive patterns of thought, and the goal which each aims to reach.

THE ONTOLOGICAL JOURNEY

In charting this journey, I shall rely primarily on Augustine's thought and the tradition he established rather than on Anselm's ontological argument, since, as was noted previously, the transformation brought about by Anselm, the compressing, as it were, of the basic outlook into the one and supposedly all-significant argument, had the effect of over-shadowing the full dimensions of the form of spirituality he represented.[4] To begin with, the intellectual milieu of Augustine's thought is that of Neoplatonism, with its emphasis on the self and self-knowledge through a dialectical leading of the mind to an apprehension of reality and truth. The starting-point of the ontological journey, one that leaves its mark on every stage of the way, is the self and its reflections on itself reaching upward to the ultimate relation to God. The Biblical watchword, often repeated, was "Arise, O my soul, enter the inner chamber of thy mind, and shut out all thoughts, save that of God alone." We know the force of this starting-point for Augustine from the famous question and response recorded in the *Soliloquia*. There, Reason asks Augustine what it is that he most wants to know, and he answers, "God and the Soul." To Reason's further question, "Nothing else?," Augustine answers, "Absolutely nothing." This subordination, if not exclusion, of the *world* was to have fateful consequences centuries later, when scientific study of the world replaced the pseudo-sciences into which the idea of the world as a system of signs and symbols had degenerated. For Augustine, of course, did not totally exclude the world, but saw it, as indeed he saw all things, as similitudes and likenesses capable of leading the mind to God. The centrality of the soul and God, however, remained, and, as is well known, Augustine was critical of excursions into explanations of the things in the world because he regarded them as distractions from what should be the main concern—God and the Soul.

Mirroring his own personal odyssey as described in the *Confessions*, Augustine set out especially in *De Trinitate* to uncover through a meditative dialectic, leading the mind by reasoned steps, the *presence* in the soul of the Uncreated Light or the Light in which everything finite is understood. This task forms the essence of the ontological way, and it is conditioned in three decisive ways: first, by the starting-point in the soul; secondly, by the distinction between *Sapientia* and *Scientia* and the rational, dialectical ascent to this wisdom in the form of *understanding*; and, finally, by the conception of God as Truth (*De Trin.* VIII, 2) embracing *Bonum* and *Esse* as well, the transcendentals of later Scholasticism. I should like now to consider how each of these conditions figures in the outworking of the ontological way.

In starting with the soul, often called the "mind" in his writings, Augustine was well aware that he was dealing with a finite and created reality, a fact that was later obscured by those who expressed their uneasiness over what came to be called, pejoratively, "illuminationism," because they believed it meant the abolishing of the gap between the Creator and the creature. I regard this as an error; "God is above the mind," he wrote (*De Trin.* XV, 1), and what is above us is a nature not *created* but *creating*. Augustine never failed to note the difference between the two natures, and from all he wrote it is clear that he was acutely aware of the fact that the human mind is a *medium*, an other, and that in whatever way God may be present in that other, that presence will be conditioned by the nature of the created medium itself. In short, the divine presence is manifested to the limit of the particular medium in which it is present. This condition does not limit God in any sense; on the contrary, God may be presumed to know the limitation imposed by his own creation, which is to say that there is a divine recognition of the difference between the soul and the world—both of which are creatures. Soul manifests what the soul can manifest, and world manifests what the world can manifest; the only asymmetry as between the two media which might be assumed is that we have more direct access to, or may know better, the soul than the world around us, but this asymmetry is not to be taken for granted as something absolute and unqualified. Self-deception enters more readily into our efforts at self-knowledge than it is likely to do in the case of our inquiries into the nature of physical reality. Augustine was well aware of this fact, something that can be seen in the well-known passage from the *Confessions* where he says, "I thought myself more myself in what I approved in myself than in what I disapproved."

The element of immediacy to be found in Augustine's approach is attached most directly to the knowledge that the mind has of itself. "Whoever seeks to inquire," he writes, "*wills* to know" (*De Trin.* IX, 12), and is aware of that determination about itself. Every mind, moreover, is said to know with certainty three things—that it *understands*, that it *is*, and that it *lives*. While, to be sure, a reflective awareness is required for an apprehension of these three things, they form the starting-point for the inquiry, and Augustine does not regard them as the result of reasoning or as involving the dialectical ascent to God that is clearly evident in the quest for the Divine Presence. As I shall suggest, whatever immediacy of apprehension may be found at the end of the quest is, not unlike Hegel's conception, a mediated immediacy, the result of the mind's having been led to its destination through a rational process.

Starting with the soul or mind was, of course, no arbitrary beginning, but rather one suggested, not only by the meditative approach as such, but more importantly by the religious conception of man's having been made in the image of God. It is, however, of great importance to notice that, for Augustine, that image is not simply to be identified with the mind as the power that distinguishes human beings from the things and animals of creation, but rather with that part of the mind capable of contemplating the eternal truths whereby the mind judges corporeal things (*De Trin.* XII, 4; cf. XII, 1). And indeed it is the recovery of these truths—truths, that is, whose existence has been there all along—which is at the same time the recovery of the Divine Presence or the Uncreated Light. The question now is, how does this journey take place?

Two conceptions absolutely essential for the quest are, first, the idea of *understanding* and the sort of intelligibility this represents, and, second, the idea of *Sapientia* and its distinction from *Scientia*. To begin with the idea of understanding and the formula "faith seeking understanding," let me say that, while I believe I understand what Augustine meant, I do not regard his meaning as either obvious or without ambiguity. The quest for understanding faith is essentially coupled with the *credo ut intelligam*—"I believe in order that I may understand"—formula; as Augustine says, "For we believe in order that we may know, we do not know in order that we may believe . . ." (*Tract. Gospel of John* XL, 9). Faith here has two closely related senses. On the one hand, it is faith as *content*, or the Christian understanding of God, man, and world contained in the sacred writings. On the other hand, faith means the relation of the individual to that content and to the God disclosed in it; at the outset one accepts it as true and is willing to trust it as a guide for life. "When," says Augustine, "the mind has been imbued with the first elements of that faith which worketh by love [Gal. 5:6], it endeavors by *purity of life* to attain unto sight . . ." (*Enchiridion* I, 5; italics added). Faith thus has its *cognitive* side expressed in the acceptance of the content as true; if, however, that is to be more than a "mere assent," there must be a *conative* side that involves love and trust, the will to shape life in accordance with that content, so that in the end "he who wills to do the Father's will, shall know" (John 7:17).[5] It is with both aspects of faith in mind that Augustine engages in the process of understanding, the best model for which is found in *De Trinitate* (see IX, 1.1).

The question naturally arising at this point is, exactly what is meant by understanding and what contribution does it make to the religious relationship? Two pairs of distinctions are needed at this point. We must distinguish, first, between the sort of intelligibility represented by understanding that stems from the dialectical procedure of the Platonic tradition and proof or demonstration as represented by the logical tradition stemming from Aristotle via Boethius. Secondly, we must take into account the difference between the work of reason *within* faith and that same work as it figures *prior* to faith. Augustine's version of the ontological journey clearly means a quest for intelligibility in which finite things and experiences—including the knowledge of the mind itself—

("things below") are seen as means whereby the mind is led to grasp the transcendent truths ("things above").[6] We are not to think of this process as a "natural theology" based on a demonstrative reason of wholly human proportions, since, according to the formula *"in lumine tuo videbimus lumen,"* all understanding comes through the illumination of the uncreated light. The emphasis falls instead on the manner in which the finite and created things serve as symbols and signs through which the divine presence can be understood. Our only access to the meaning of a content that transcends man is by finding likeness of it in the knowledge of created things, but especially in the human mind. The mind is led through a series of steps to understand.

This reflective and meditative approach, which each, in the end, must trace out for him- or herself, represents something quite different from a form of logical demonstration in which propositions are related to each other in accordance with explicitly stated principles that determine the conclusion and its validity. This objectified pattern of intelligibility, which, for a number of important historical reasons, came to supplant the ontological way, can be grasped by the intellect through conceptualization of the terms and logical principles without any reference to the inner experience of any individual. As I shall point out later on, the demonstrative approach has its own appropriateness for the cosmological starting-point, although I shall propose that it can be understood in a way that overcomes a familiar difficulty. If the way of inference is understood merely as the logical movement from what is *present* —the world and its features—to what is *absent*, or the God at the end of the syllogism, then God appears as the reality wholly external and beyond, the reality we have in no sense met before, symbolized by Tillich's idea of meeting a Stranger. I shall return to this point in due course; for the present the main point I wish to make is that, as previously noted, it is a mistake to distinguish and oppose the two ways by interpreting the cosmological as wholly inferential. Each represents a pattern of intelligibility, but the patterns are different, and the task is to recognize that fact and then seek to determine how they can be understood as aiming at the same reality.

There are passages in Augustine that adumbrate the familiar demonstrative proofs for God, but if we attend to *De Trinitate*, which is his most sustained effort at faith seeking understanding, we find, not a logical demonstration of the existence of the Trinitarian God, but a reflective recovery in the mind of several trinities of the soul that are *similitudes* of the true God. He does not start with the likenesses and deduce the Trinity; on the contrary, he starts with the doctrine of the Trinity and shows how, through a reflective analysis of the experience of ourselves, it becomes intelligible to speak of God as a trinity or community of persons. The result is not a discovery of the content of faith itself, but, rather, the rational apprehension that the content is intelligible. What contribution, then, does this understanding make, since it clearly represents an advance beyond our original position? The answer is that there are two contributions: first, understanding serves as a spur to seeking God; second, it has the power of confirming the believer in his faith. "And yet again," Augustine writes,

> understanding still seeks him whom it finds: for "God looked down upon the sons of men," as it is sung in the holy psalm, "to see if there were any that would understand, and seek after God." And man, therefore, ought for this purpose to have understanding that he may seek after God
> [*De Trin.* XV, 2.2].

The quest for understanding is not to be seen as a journey leading away from the object of faith to some land of abstract speculation; on the contrary, according to Augustine, we are able to seek after what we already in some sense know. "For it would seem clear," he writes in the *Confessions*, "that no one can call upon thee without knowing thee, for if he did he might invoke another than thee, knowing thee not" (*Confessions* I, 1; cf. V, 3 [trans. Sheed]). The second contribution of understanding is equally clear; it provides what we may call *confirming reasons* in the rational dialectic, whereby the intelligibility of faith is seen, so that, as Augustine says, we avoid saying foolish and superstitious things over which the heathen cannot hold their sides from laughing!

It remains to mention at least two places in Augustine's writings where reason is said to *precede* the ambience of faith. The first is in *De Ordine,* an early work to be sure, where he says, "In point of time, authority, i.e., faith, is first; but in the order of reality, reason is prior" (*De Ord.* II, 9.26). And the point of this reversal is explained in words from Letter 120: "So, therefore, if it is rational that faith precedes reason in the case of certain great matters that cannot be grasped there cannot be the least doubt that *reason which persuades us of this precept*—that faith precedes reason—*itself precedes faith.*"[7] The precept, in short, has roots in reason itself, and is thus not entirely dependent on the passage in the Book of Isaiah from which it comes, a point that receives further support from the fact that in *De Utilitate Credendi,* Augustine argues for the validity of *credo ut intelligam* against those who opposed it. The point I wish to stress here is that the presence of reason both within and beyond faith represents a distinctive pattern of intelligibility in the ontological way, but one which is not accurately described in terms of immediacy and self-evidence alone. It is quite likely that Thomas' interpretation of the ontological *argument* as requiring an appeal to self-evidence led to the characterization of what I am calling the ontological journey in terms of immediacy in contrast to his own decidedly inferential approach.

What, then, is the goal of the process of understanding? The ultimate answer is, of course, God as Truth; the proximate answer is wisdom or *Sapientia.* Time and again, Augustine invoked the distinction between *Sapientia* and *Scientia* as fundamental to his quest. For it is *Sapientia*—the contemplation or intellectual cognition of eternal things, the first principles of Being, Truth and God, along with the mathematical truths and the rational proportions of music—which represents the image of God in that part of the mind which contemplates them. *Scientia*, by contrast, is rational cognition of temporal things, wherein the mind judges these things according to incorporeal and eternal reasons.

The crux of the ontological journey appears at this point; the apprehension of *Sapientia is* the recovery of the Divine Presence in the soul, as the final books of the *De Trinitate* make abundantly clear. As I pointed out previously, however, this is a mediated presence in a creature who is finite—a feature underlined by Augustine in his own delicate way when he says that the gulf between the Creator and the creature is not spanned because, among other things, we forget, whereas God never does! God, moreover, is present only in accordance with the nature of the soul and thus at the same time transcends that presence, since, as Augustine says, "There is the greatest possible unlikeness between our word and knowledge and the Divine word and knowledge" (*De Trin.* XV, 11). And the difference between the Creator and man is underlined again at the central point where he speaks of God's image in man becoming tarnished and defaced by sin, so that it needs to be renewed, except that it can be renewed *only* by Him who first formed it, "for that image cannot form itself again, as it could deform itself" (*De Trin.* XIV, 16). Despite the unlikeness, however, the Divine Presence is affirmed, and that is the rock upon which the ontological way rests.

Augustine was well aware of the extent to which his entire venture depends on the conception of God as Truth: Truth, however, not in the logical or epistemological sense in which it is attached as a characteristic to a proposition, but in the sense of the Being or reality and the Good of things in their truth. It is, of course, the loss of this conception of Truth— Hegel was the last great representative of it—which makes the recovery of the Augustinian tradition difficult in the present age, for if truth is no more than a feature assimilated to human knowledge seen as standing over against reality, it can no longer be seen as the Divine Presence. Augustine was, moreover, mindful of the obstacles standing in the way of apprehending clearly what Truth in this sense means, and he knew well that we are far more successful in grasping the particular truths that make up *Scientia* than we are in articulating the substance of *Sapientia*. "It is written," says Augustine, "that 'God is light'; not in such ways as these eyes see, but in such way as the heart sees, where it is said, He is truth." And, he continues, "ask not what is truth; for immediately the darkness of corporeal images and the clouds of phantasm will put themselves in the way, and will disturb that calm which at the first twinkling shone forth to thee, when I said truth. See that thou remainest, if thou canst, in that first twinkling . . ." (*De Trin.* VIII, 2). I purposely close this account of the ontological journey on this quasi-mystical note because I want to call attention to the fact that it is not *presumptive* with respect to the knowledge of God possible for finite beings; the Divine Presence, on this approach, does not preclude the transcendence of God, which, I take it, was the chief anxiety behind the objections of those who characterized the ontological way as "illuminationism" in a pejorative sense.

THE COSMOLOGICAL JOURNEY

That a new way of approach should have developed, starting not with the self but with the world, is understandable in the light of certain changes in the philosophical and theological climate that took place in the period between the death of Anselm and the middle of the thirteenth century. During this time the full body of Aristotle's writings became available in the West, and this meant that, in addition to his logical writings introduced earlier, there were on hand the *Metaphysics* and other works in natural philosophy, especially the *Physics*, which Hegel rightly described as less a physics than a comprehensive philosophy of nature. It was no longer possible to restrict attention, as Augustine had done, to God and the Soul, because the world of nature was thrust upon the scene with a new prominence. It was, moreover, no longer possible to view this world, as Augustinians had done, exclusively in terms of signs and symbols serving to lead the mind to God.

The world now appeared as having a new and more insistent *actuality* as an interrelated system of things and processes structured according to genera and species, distinctive levels of being and regular cycles of events and developments. In addition, a new pattern of intelligibility emerged, quite different from the meditative dialectic of the Augustinians; emphasis was now placed on the analysis of all things in terms of Aristotle's four αἰτίαι—causes and reasons—and of his demonstrative logic aimed at providing proof.

It was this new apprehension of the world and this new way of reasoning both within it and about it that filled the mind of Thomas Aquinas and prompted him to set out on the cosmological journey. The starting-point could no longer be the inner character of the mind, but rather a fastening of attention on the *existence* of the world and its distinctive generic features for the purpose of showing that it is not self-supporting, that it does not have its ground in any of its proper parts, but is in fact dependent on a transcendent power. Accordingly, Thomas set forth his well-known proofs for the existence of God, availing himself of the manifest existence of the world and its structure together with the principle of causality and the illegitimacy of the infinite regress. I need not rehearse these arguments for present purposes, for they are indeed far better known at present than the Augustinian dialectic, which is the reason I dwelt so long on developing its meaning; I wish instead to propose a basic notion in terms of which they can be reinterpreted, so as to close the gap between the two ways and at the same time to offer a response to the often repeated religious charge against the cosmological way, which says that it yields no more than the God at the end of the syllogism.

Before coming to my proposal, however, I must call attention to several of the grounds on which Thomas set aside the ontological way. There is, of course, his rejection of the formal ontological argument, but I am less concerned with that than with some underlying features of his thought as they bear on what I have been calling the ontological way. The first is his claim that the first principles of *Sapientia* have no special status and are no more than finite structures of the created intellect. This claim effectively obscures the distinction between *Sapientia* and *Scientia* and places all contents of the mind on the same level, which in time came to mean that *Scientia* covers the whole ground and both philosophy and theology are put in jeopardy. Anyone who is concerned today for the preservation of philosophy knows full well the consequences of that reduction. But, further, the leveling of *Sapientia* meant a denial of the divine presence or the Uncreated Light in the soul, prompted by the belief that the only way of approach to God must be through what exists and is better known to us—namely, the world. Thomas, moreover, ever cautious in his treatment of Augustine, nevertheless drove a further wedge between them when he declared that, whereas Truth identified as the Being of God may be evident, *a* primal truth is not, and, therefore, it is necessary to argue for the existence of such *a* truth via the cosmological route. I cannot consider here the problem posed by this nose-in-the-tent nominalism beyond saying that I believe Hartshorne is right in holding that God is *the* being, *the* individual, and that this is the appropriate identification. I can, however, join the issue presented by the emphasis on existence, and introduce more explicitly the concept of *Presence* as a reconciling idea.

Consider for a start that, throughout the entire Biblical literature, the reality of God is manifest over and again as *Presence* in a medium or other which, though the bearer of that Presence, is not identical with it, and hence God was seen as at the same time transcending that other in every dimension. This model of *presence in* and *transcendence of* the medium is found in every Biblical theophany from the burning bush of Moses through Isaiah's encounter with the Holy—"In the year that King Uzziah died, I saw the Lord ..." —to the Mount of Transfiguration, and it is recapitulated in Christ, although this is admittedly a special case because of the need to understand how the Presence can be total. But leaving that explicitly theological problem to one side, the basic model of presence and transcendence remains as a viable one for philosophical understanding. Suppose we were to reconsider the cosmological way from the standpoint of this model and ask whether the arguments may not be seen as a way of leading the mind by some logical constraints to discover the *presence* of God in the cosmos. From this vantage point it would no longer be a matter of arguing from a present existence to a God who is absent and, as the charge goes, is merely inferred—a "must be" God—but rather of arguing from the fact and the surface features of the world to the *presence* in it at its depth of the God who called it forth. In so reinterpreting the situation it would be essential to recover the full dimensions of the concept of causality involved in the cosmological way. The tendency to identify the concept with efficient causality in a pre-eminent sense obscures the other factors initially present in Aristotle's four questions about every process, but especially significant is the loss or subordination of what was traditionally known as the *formal* cause, or that reason which points to presence. Inferring one existent as necessary for accounting for another, if viewed as a matter of externally related realities, fails utterly to show how the independent ground *informs* or is *present* in the reality to which it gives rise. The abstract conception of causality, moreover, according to which it is merely a sequence, obscures the genuine immanence of the *maker* in the product made, as if the so-called cause had to be over and finished before the so-called effect could take place, as if the cause could vanish without a trace of itself to be found in the effect. Even in finite creativity we are aware of this immanence of the poet, the painter, the philosopher, the theologian in what each brings forth, and it finds current expression in Whitehead's concept of *ingression*. The cosmological way, in short, is the way of showing the presence of God in the world serving as a medium of disclosure. As we saw in considering the ontological way, however, that presence is to be understood in terms of the capacity of the medium to bear it, and hence each way will disclose what is appropriate to its own primary medium. It was for this reason that Bonaventure distinguished between the presence of God in the *image* that is man, and in the *traces* to be found in the natural order. Should it not be obvious that both ways are needed, and, were we left with either alone, we would be the poorer for it?

To see the cosmological way as a quest for presence overcomes the externality that attaches to an inference to what is absent, and at the same time turns the edge of the objection that this way ends in a must-be God whom we do not really meet. And if it be thought that some sense of meeting or encountering presence has no vital importance or is reserved exclusively for the out-and-out mystical way, let me close by reminding you of what Anselm had to say on the matter. There can be no question that Anselm's argument as such represents the *ne plus ultra* of rationalism, regardless of whether one takes it to be sound or not. There are, however, two passages in the *Proslogion* which I find remarkable both in themselves and in the fact that they seem to have been totally ignored. In the midst of his meditating on the divine necessity, Anselm arrests himself, so to speak, and says, "O, Lord, if Thou art so necessary, how is it that I do not *experience* Thee?"—*Te non sentio*. And he repeats the same idea in slightly different language two sections farther along. What is this question if it is not the expression of the need for *presence* and of the sense that there is something abstract and incomplete about the "must-be" God standing apart from some concrete medium of disclosure? Necessity always seems so secure and overpowering, but there are times when it is too much. If I understand anything at all about modern skepticism in the face of religious truth it is that the critical question posed is not whether God *must be*, but whether God *is*. It is for this reason that I have sought to close the gap between the two ways by proposing that both can be seen, each in its own way, and not reducible to the other, as a journey to the *Divine Presence*.

NOTES

1. *De Trinitate*, XV, 3; italics added.
2. Paul Tillich, "Two Types of Philosophy of Religion," in *Theology of Culture*, ed. Robert C. Kimball (New York: Oxford University Press, 1959), pp. 10–29.
3. See *St. Anselm's Proslogion*, trans. H. J. Charlesworth (Oxford: Clarendon Press, 1965), pp. 23ff.
4. This restriction is not meant to deny that Anselm belonged to the meditative rationality of the Augustinian tradition. If evidence is needed, one has but to point to Anselm's own hesitation about whether he should write down the proof and thus "objectify" it or whether it was best left in a meditative form requiring each individual to confront the thoughts in his own mind.
5. See *Tract. Gospel of John* XXXIX, 6, where Augustine interprets this verse in terms of the "believe that you may understand" formula.
6. See *De Trin.* I, 1.
7. Charlesworth (n. 3, above), p. 27.

COMMENTS

by

W. Norris Clarke, s.j.

COMMENT ON
PROFESSOR CAPUTO'S PAPER

I am deeply appreciative of John Caputo's paper, on two counts: first, as a distinguished philosophical contribution in its own right; secondly, as a stimulating challenge to the type of systematic metaphysics I have laid out in my main address. On the first count, I find his phenomenological description, or better, interpretation, of the human face both deeply insightful and at times deeply moving. It seems to me almost a paradigm case of what phenomenology—in particular what I might call hermeneutical phenomenology—can do at its best. The human face is indeed, as he so eloquently displays, a surface, a surface over an abyss. And the abyss that it opens up on is indeed a mystery, or includes within it a mystery, that resists sounding by conceptual intelligence. This is where straight description falls short, and interpretation must come into play. And I think he is right that there is probably no more powerful example of Heidegger's characterization of being as always both revealing and concealing. The human person is pre-eminently the locus of both at once. And herein lies the difficulty. For the mystery at first approach remains cloaked in ambiguity; it can enclose a mystery of light, opening to a higher transcendence, or a mystery of darkness, a meaningless void. Professor Caputo very cagily refuses to tell us how to go about resolving the ambiguity. He wants us to experience the mystery and dwell within it first. Fine! But I do not think one can stay indefinitely in this ambiguity; one must break out sooner or later. The question is, how?

This is where the profound challenge to my own way of doing metaphysics—and with it, of course, that of St. Thomas and the whole classical tradition—comes in. I lay out, or better, unfold, a whole systematic metaphysics of being *as intel-*

ligible, which exhibits a powerful overarching integration and harmony in its large lines. It is thus what I might call a metaphysics of light rather than of darkness. But what if the very radical experience of being itself, not only of my own personal being with its uniquely expressive medium, the face, but of every being, and of the cosmos as a whole, at least as I experience it, is similarly both a revelation and a concealment, covering over an abyss that is an unsoundable mystery, whose potential interpretation hovers ambiguously between light and darkness, intelligibility and absurdity? How then get started in my metaphysics of intelligibility, of light, at all? A fine question, and not a simple one to answer. The great modern "Masters of Suspicion," as they have been called, all thrust in to have their say here: Nietzsche (no objective truth—will power has the deciding voice), Marx (most men are alienated from their true humanity by inhuman economics), Freud (the surface is not what it seems: the true motivations may be unconscious), Derrida and the Deconstructionists (every positive text can be dissolved into its contrary or shadow text, and the author, too).

I am quite willing to concede that one does not come to metaphysical thinking with an absolutely naked and pure intellect, to read off the deep structure of the universe by a necessary logical necessity free of any lurking shadows of ambiguity. There must indeed be a whole pre-philosophical, positive, lived contact with and experience of being. I think one must taste, so to speak, successful runs of intelligibility through the experience of something like science or more basically the practical making and repairing of things. One must experience the goodness of being through close observational contact with good people who live the good life, and show forth its fruits to our intuitive empathy. What Aristotle claimed as necessary for the intelligent doing of ethics may well be true in its own way for metaphysics.

It may well be true, as many claim, that our basic attitude toward being is determined in a way difficult to displace during the first few years of a child's life, even the first eighteen months, as some claim. Its parents (or substitute parents) are for it like a paradigm of reality as a whole: if they are loving, caring, reliable, assisting it sincerely to grow, then reality as a whole will appear as potentially a positive, good place to be, full of potentiality for growth. If they are the opposite, then reality as a whole will appear as a dangerous, ambiguous, threatening place, so that the safest tactic is to draw back in fear and not trust it, lest one get hurt even more. A social matrix is thus needed first in order to make possible and nurture a positive initial experience of being as basically ordered, intelligible, filled with much actual goodness and potential fulfillment.[1] Probably a whole supporting culture is needed, or at least a group larger than the family.[2] Yes, we must first live well if we are to philosophize well. I do not believe that any part of philosophy, including metaphysics, can begin in a rationalist way from pure abstract concepts with conclusions drawn deductively from them, as Spinoza seemed to wish. I think it must be a reflection on a primary level of lived experience, seeking to illuminate this experience in depth and set it in a vision of the whole. But if the experience is *predominantly* distorted, truncated, disordered, rotten, so to speak, it will be almost impossible to illuminate it in depth with integral intelligibility, unless someone comes to lift the veil onto something more positive. Reality must somehow reveal itself as *implicitly* ordered, intelligible, good, fulfilling, before we can *explicitly* weave it together in a metaphysical system.

But because a social support is needed for a rich enough, positive enough experience of being to support an integrating metaphysical system, it does not follow that the social community is merely projecting its own positive view of reality as pure wishful thinking out of a void and onto a void. I think it rather makes possible and leads us to a partial unveiling of the positivity of being underlying its mysterious face or sur-face, so that we become sufficiently aware by connatural sympathetic resonance (knowledge by connaturality, as St. Thomas would put it) of the presence of the great "transcendental properties" of all being, that it is somehow one, active, intelligible, good, and beautiful. Then we can draw these out and follow their natural lines of force to weave them together into an integral metaphysical vision. But unfortunately there are no logical or metaphysical rules for successfully bringing about the initial positive experience of being. In my judgment (coming out of my long experience and reflection on it), the basic experiences of friendship and love, and of shared play and creativity, are, despite accompanying shadows, so positive and revelatory of being that no lurking subconscious or dimension of alienation can substantially subvert, distort, or dissolve them. Nor have Nietzsche, Marx, Freud, or Derrida ever come near to giving any convincing evidence to the contrary. But I am quite willing to admit with John Caputo that there is a pre-conceptual, pre-metaphysical depth to our experience of being as mystery, whose initial ambiguity, however, can be sufficiently illuminated by a pre-conceptual, connatural mode of knowing, loving, and acting; and there is a post-conceptual mystery of being as superabundant light at the end of our conceptual metaphysical journey when we emerge, it is hoped, into vision and at-one-ment. But extending across between the two mysteries it is good, I am convinced, to have a solid, though swaying, bridge of sturdy, well-woven metaphysical cords.

I might add that, in my own systematic structure, positive and optimistic though the overall lines are, there is a definite place where ambiguity and the shadow of evil enter in most appropriately. This is in the nature of *finite action*, in a being on the journey of the Great Circle of Being. Action is, indeed, the place where being is both revealed and concealed, as Heidegger saw and said so well. But despite the basic goodness, orderliness, and harmony of being, each finite being is an act of existence imitating the divine, but mixed in with a limiting element, which means a partial negation, almost a kind of infection by non-being, a shadow element. As a result, there tends to be, most especially in free beings like ourselves, but perhaps even to some extent in all beings in some slight way, a mysterious and unpredictable instability in being and goodness, a kind of drift toward non-being, which needs to be watched over and healed by a higher Providence. This mystery dimension of darkness, of the shadow of nothingness, in being, is not one that can be conceptually probed and reduced to reason; to attempt to do so would be, as St. Augustine said of evil, "like trying to see darkness or hear silence." Thus in the last analysis the journey along the Great Circle of Being is well enough lit up so that we can see clearly enough the large outlines and make our way along with enough security and confidence, even joy, for our needs, but yet always accompanied by the sometimes thicker, sometimes thinner shadow side of finite being, with its not always stable mixture of the "yes" of the light and energy of existence and the "no" of limitation, negation, and non-being. Thanks to John Caputo for gently forcing us to bring more into focus the shadow side of being.

NOTES

1. As Gregory Baum puts it well, in *Man Becoming* (New York: Herder & Herder, 1970): "In general it is the love and care offered to us by others that create in us the strength to enter into the dialogue of life. Only as we are loved and recognized do we gain the self-confidence necessary to listen and reply. . . . Love, in other words, gives freedom. . . . This strength comes from a certain self-possession to which men have access only if they have shared life or enjoyed communion with others. . . . The love we receive prepares us to give love to others. . . . A man needs others, because by extending his friendship and love to them and by bearing the burden with them in love, he is in fact becoming more truly himself" (pp. 49–50, 53).

2. It should be clear how powerfully supportive a role can be played by a *positive* religious vision (it does not seem that *all* religious visions do in fact support or encourage a metaphysical structure of thinking). This was certainly true of the medievals, such as St. Thomas. Some would hold that this is always implicitly the case, and that only within such supra-philosophical vision can

we find enough strength and hope to trust our natural intelligence and thus work out a philosophical world vision. This is too complex and difficult a question to enter into here. Aristotle might be cited as an exception.

COMMENT ON
PROFESSOR FORD'S PAPER

I am grateful to Lewis Ford for pushing me, in his paper, to think out my own position more consistently and adequately than I have up to this point. I admire his almost legendary tenacity and patience in following up on a discussion, pushing hard on any ambiguous points, trying to bring every aspect out into the clear, not allowing anyone to hide in some conveniently vague corner. He has done that here again to me, and in the process has also unveiled some rather surprising new developments or adaptations in his own position. Hence his statement here is important for the history of his own thought and not merely for mine.

The first point he pushes me on is my attempt to distinguish between the dimension of intentional being in God, or the contents of the divine field of consciousness with respect to creatures in their changing history, and the intrinsic real being of God, which I maintained was not affected by His relational consciousness. Lewis Ford does not think it possible or that helpful to draw such a sharp distinction between these two aspects of the divine being. At least he does not think I can consistently do it and still hold on, as a Thomist, to the immutability of the inner real being of God, and this for two reasons: (1) the Thomistic insistence on the absolute simplicity of God undercuts any such distinction—God's consciousness *is* His being, and anything that affects His consciousness would have to affect His being too; and (2) from a process point of view, the conscious life of God is the most important thing about Him, and anything that affected and enriched the conscious life of God would be worthless if it did not affect and enrich His inner real being too.

Lewis Ford uses the strong attack on my concessions to

process thought from another understandably concerned Thomist, Professor Kondoleon of Villanova University, to try to smoke me out and get me to make further decisions.[1] But he also in the process puts his finger very tellingly, it seems to me, on the weak spot in Kondoleon's position when the latter is forced to concede that the consciousness of God would have to be *different*—though not thereby changing—because He decided to create this world rather than some other or none at all. And it would have to be different not only because of God's own unilateral decision to create—this difference, of course, would not necessarily involve change, as I have often pointed out myself—but also because of the responses that His free creatures actually make in time to His creative love.

Under the pressure of Lewis Ford's critique I have come to the conclusion—an indication, by the way, that philosophers actually do listen to each other, at least occasionally—that I should tone down my previous perhaps too sharp distinction between the intentional or consciousness dimension of God's life and His immutable intrinsic real being. I think it closer to the truth to say that God's inner being is indeed affected by His "extroverted" life of consciousness with respect to creatures. In consequence I would have to qualify again, a little more precisely, the immutability of God. I think that one can certainly say, and should definitely say, at least this much: there is an *absolute* (non-relative) dimension of the divine being that is indeed affected but not in any *absolute* way, by His relations to His creatures because it is by nature prior to and independent of any particular creation. That is the inner inexhaustible abyss, or infinite plenitude, of God's creative power, His luminous intellectual power, and the constant actual exercise of it in His eternal self-consciousness and enjoyment of His own immensely rich interior life (the conscious, loving "circuminsession" of His Trinitarian life), etc. This eternal inner plenitude of power and life is not affected in any *absolute* way by the relations to His creatures, but is affected precisely in the *relative* way proper to extroverted consciousness, to personal being's relations to its *other*. So

God's whole being, including His absolute being, is indeed affected by all of His conscious life (both knowledge and love), but in some respects both absolutely and relatively (i.e., the eternal inner perfection of His nature independent of creatures plus the eternal interpersonal relations between the three Divine Persons), in other respects absolutely and not relatively (i.e., the eternal inner perfection of the divine nature in itself), and in other respects relatively and not absolutely (i.e., His extroverted knowledge and love relations with creatures).

But would not this imply that in the case of the absolute nature of God being affected relatively to His creatures there would be some real accidental change in God, some real composition of substance and accident that would contradict the divine simplicity? No, I do not think so. For in Aristotelian–Thomistic real accidental change there is always a change in the *absolute* (non-relative) being of the substance or subject of the change. Either the new accident itself is something of the absolute order; or, if the accident is a relation, for a real change and real composition there must be some foundation for the change within the subject in the *absolute* order. But in our present case of the relation of the absolute being of God to His relations with respect to creatures, nothing new in the absolute order is added or affected in the inner being of God. For whatever God knows with respect to creatures is only a limited participation in His own already infinite perfection; whatever return of love a creature makes to Him is only a new explicit unfolding of the active potentiality which God's creative power and knowledge put into it in the first place; so it neither augments nor raises to a higher absolute level the absolute perfection already there. In a word, there is a relative enrichment, if you will, but not an absolute one. As a result, there is no *Aristotelian* real change or real composition in Him. It should always be remembered that there is one dimension of the divine being that has traditionally been allowed to transcend, without negating, the simplicity of the absolute being of God—namely, that of *relations*. Although

COMMENTS

many process thinkers do not seem aware of this, any denial of
this point would render impossible the inner Trinitarian life
of God that consists entirely of *relations*, and real ones at that.
Thus both the immutability and simplicity of God are not
completely "atomic" absolute attributes totally intelligible
without reference to the other attributes of God, in particular
the great central controlling one of perfect *personal* being.
If this brings me somewhat closer to Whitehead's own distinction between the primordial and the consequent nature of
God, reinterpreted as absolute and relative, so much the better. It is in this context that I would like to set what I have
said elsewhere about its being possible and necessary to say
that in some positive way God's eternal absolute joy is "enhanced," as Ford likes to put it, by the loving responses of
His creatures, and that He experiences something like com-
passion at their rejection of His love. I think this distinction
between absolute and relative dimensions in God's unified
being a more apt way of putting it than Hartshorne's solution,
which Ford favors, of speaking of the inner primordial core of
God's being as "static," and hence "abstract" as compared to
the actual existential life of the divine consciousness as related
to the world. The intense inner life of God, though not changing, is the furthest thing from "static."

After this concession I should inject a modest critical note.
At one point in his paper Lewis Ford, while criticizing the
"timeless" view of divine knowledge as eternal, repeats again
the old and often dissolved objection that "Were God to
know the entire course of the world's events in a single timeless act, such knowledge could be regarded as immutable and
necessary, but at the expense of depriving the world of any
contingency, since what is immutably and certainly known
cannot be otherwise." As has so often been shown, this is a
confusion in modal logic. The proper location of the modal
term "necessary" must be as follows: If God timelessly knows
event X, then it is *necessarily true* that this will happen at its
appropriate time (i.e., necessity *de dicto*); it does not follow
that event X will *happen necessarily* (i.e., necessity *de re*). God

162

knows the event *because it happens,* because He sees it as happening, from His eternal Now; it does not happen *because He knows it.* This particular wandering ghost should be laid to rest once for all, it seems to me.

I cannot pass over another small point, a quotation that Lewis Ford draws from a 1973 article of mine, "A New Look at the Immutability of God": "For it cannot be an imperfection not to know what is not in itself knowable—i.e., the future, the not yet real, at least in its free or not yet determined aspects. Perfect knowledge of an evolving reality would by nature have to evolve with its object."[2] I was surprised at first that I had said it, but I did. It was in the context of expounding two views of divine eternity, however: one, the non-durational, timeless eternity, which St. Thomas certainly held; the other, the durational eternity, everlasting but able to evolve across the passage of time, which is the view of process thinkers and not a few other Christian philosophers and theologians, predominantly Protestant, it seems.

The above quote of mine was put forward as *from within* the second view. My position was that *both* views seemed to me to be tenable, *orthodox* theistic and Christian ones, although the second was certainly not *traditional,* at least in the main Thomistic tradition. I said that I was now "leaning" a little more toward the second, but had not yet firmly made up my mind, and was definitely unwilling to rule out the traditional one. I still think this question so plunged in mystery that we should allow both positions to co-exist with tolerance inside the philosophy and theology of God. I am still moved by the remarkable statement of A. H. Armstrong, the great Plotinus scholar and also Christian, usually an ardent defender of the Plotinian timeless view, when he wondered "whether non-durational eternity is a concept that can be usefully employed in any philosophical or theological context."[3] It now seems to me, however, that my above statement is too strong; on the particular point involved, I do not think one can make any tight argument, as is implied there, that all knowledge of an evolving reality, even free, must itself be evolving. So I would wish this quotation to be left behind, buried in the sand, so to speak, of my own evolving thought.

Nonetheless, I will admit that I have recently cooled a little toward St. Thomas' uncompromising view on God's absolutely timeless and process-less knowledge of all futures. The occasion was a remarkable and fascinating text of St. Thomas which I ran into only recently for the first time while preparing a delivered but as yet unpublished, and, I have to admit, definitely iconoclastic paper on God's knowledge of the possibles according to St. Thomas. St. Thomas, as is well enough known, holds that God knows in a single timeless vision all the possibles distinctly as an *actually infinite multitude* (not a *number*, of course, because an infinite multitude could not be numerable—an actually infinite number would be a patent contradiction). I maintain (in the first predominantly critical article on St. Thomas I have done) that such a knowledge is impossible, because the set of all the possibles is inexhaustibly endless, unfinishable, and can never be completed in an *actually infinite* multitude seen as complete by God in a single act. For no matter how many or how great the creatures God actually makes, the gap between any finite and the infinite still remains infinite, and He can endlessly create more and better ones. So His power, His active potentiality, is infinite, but the set of distinct objective possible products of it can never be completed in an actually infinite multitude.

In the course of his analysis, however, St. Thomas brings forward a remarkable argument. He points out that there should be no difficulty in admitting that God knows an actually infinite multitude of possibles, since everyone must admit that He knows an actually infinite multitude of *actual* beings or modes of being: i.e., the blessed in heaven will live on eternally and thus continue to bring forth for unending eternity an infinite series of spiritual acts of knowing and loving. Since these are or will be all actuals, not merely possibles, and God must know them all distinctly in a single timeless act, He therefore must know an actually infinite multitude of *actuals*; and if so, there is no more problem in allowing

Him the knowledge of an actually infinite multitude of *possibles*.[4]

This, it seems to me, is a wonderful test case. Since this series will by necessity never be finished, but continue indefinitely for all eternity, it is impossible as I see it that such an endlessly growing multitude can ever be totalized in a complete set that would be *actually infinite*, hence completed, and known in a single complete act, each item being known distinctly. I think St. Thomas has been forced here by the ruthless logic of a durationless eternity and a single complete act of divine knowing into an untenable position, of demanding that God know what cannot be known—i.e., to know as completed and actual what can never become completed and actual. The set is of its nature uncompletable. Here it would seem to me that even if one holds, as I too would be quite willing to do, that God knows in an eternal Now outside and above *our kind of time* (which is determined and measured by *physical motion* in which God is not involved at all), still there would have to be some kind of internal flow and endlessly unfolding sequence in the purely spiritual intentional contents of the divine consciousness. Thus, though God's knowledge would not be involved in our kind of time flow, there would be something like a spiritual "time" flow in His consciousness in a mode proper to Him alone. I find it difficult to get around something like this, which would qualify significantly the durationless character of the divine knowing —not *our* kind of temporal duration, true, but *some* kind of spiritual duration. St. Thomas, therefore, would have done better to stick by his brilliant early solution to the problem of the divine knowledge of the possibles, when he argued that, since the pure possibles had no being to be known distinctly, God did not know them all distinctly but only the infinite indeterminate plenitude of His *active power* to make as many as He wished.[5] Sertillanges thinks that St. Thomas later joined the common tradition out of deference to the Augustinian tradition on the Divine Ideas.[6]

Before passing on to consider Lewis Ford's own daring and

radical solution of proposing that God should not be considered being at all but pure becoming, I feel I must make some reply to his charge against St. Thomas and in part me that the whole metaphysics of immutability is a purely *a priori* deduction from *a priori* first principles, as opposed to the Whiteheadian method of generalizing out of experience. If one were to deduce the immutability of God in a purely abstract way without any consideration of the term in relation with the other attributes of God, there might be just cause for complaint. But I have explicitly repudiated this purely atomic way of working out the attributes of God. And with regard to the Thomistic (and Aristotelian) metaphysics of change as requiring a cause, it should be noted that it does not at all proceed from pure *a priori* concepts or first principles. It begins with the experience and analysis of change, wherein we first notice that things that undergo real change, in the sense of acquiring something new they did not have before, *in fact* need help from another to receive this new addition; then by reflective analysis of the terms involved we get the point of the inner intelligible necessity of the connection, and then generalize to all cases of change. Thus principles such as "Whatever acquires something new it did not have before must acquire it with the help of some distinct cause" are not *a priori* first principles, but rather the *results* of analysis of experience, which *then* become principles for further conclusions and applications. The very concept itself of change is not a pure *a priori* logical one, but emerges, together with the analysis of its implications, out of the rich loam of experience. Whitehead himself, it seems to me, proceeds in a similar way when he argues that there *must* be a God, otherwise the world could have no adequate principle of order, etc. Such types of metaphysical argument are not purely *a priori*, but rather a drawing-out of the exigencies of intelligibility latent in experience itself.

Let me now turn finally to Lewis Ford's own positive suggestion for breaking out of the dilemma that God is either perfect and hence immutable being, but then not personally affected by His creatures, or that He *is* thus personally affected and responsive but then not immutable hence not perfect being. (In setting up the dilemma this way I am afraid he already unwisely concedes that absolute immutability and perfection necessarily go together, which I do not think he should concede at all—I certainly do not, in the case of the perfection of a *personal* being.) He then makes a daring new move, which seems to me a distinctly new phase in his own development: if God has to be a perfect *being*, then we have no solution; but why not say that God is not being at all but *pure becoming*? Then the same requirements for immutability, infinity, etc. would no longer hold.

Indeed a creative and daring move! But I must regretfully part company with him here. I think the price considerably too high to pay. For if God has no core of intrinsic being immutable and absolute in some way not relative to the world, then His own reality becomes totally bound up with the process of creatures and becomes almost identical with the worldly process in a kind of pantheism or strong panentheism. As he himself says, "Rather than being himself a being, God is a factor in the creation of the finite beings of the world. . . . The cessation of the beings of the world, were it possible, would also mean the termination of God's existence as becoming." (It would seem that one would have to add too that since God is *only* pure becoming, not being at all, He would then disappear from existence also—a hard saying indeed.) He also describes God as "an everlasting concrescence, that is, the growing together of all things, whether necessary or contingent, within one divine experience." It does seem to me that if God is pure becoming, not being at all but *nothing but* becoming (contrary, it seems, to Whitehead's own timeless and absolute primordial nature), and if this becoming is entirely bound up with the world's becoming, then God's existence would lose all real transcendence and become merely a factor in the world's own becoming, with no deep independent transcendence or inner life of His own. Such a God reduced to pure becoming would be definitely too immanent

COMMENTS

and too exclusively "extroverted" for my philosophical, or theological, or religious tastes. Such a God would indeed be "religiously *available*," but not transcendent enough to be the object of truly *religious* awe and adoration as Infinite Transcendent Mystery.

But it may well be that I have pushed the logic of Lewis' argument too far. So perhaps I should be content with admiring his daring from a distance without being willing to follow him. At any rate, I certainly cannot remain the same after trying to cope with his ever probing and creative mind.

NOTES

1. Theodore Kondoleon, "The Immutability of God: Some Recent Challenges," *New Scholasticism*, 13 (1973), 347–76.
2. "A New Look at the Immutability of God," in *God Knowable and Unknowable*, ed. Robert J. Roth, s.j. (New York: Fordham University Press, 1973), p. 65.
3. "Eternity, Life, and Movement in Plotinus' Accounts of *Nous*," in *Le Néoplatonisme: Colloques Internationaux, Royaumont, 1969* (Paris: Centre National de la Recherche Scientifique, 1971), p. 76.
4. *Summa Theologiae*, I, q. 14, art. 12, ad 2um: "So that which is in itself infinite can be said to be finite [*finitum*] to the knowledge of God in that it is comprehended [*comprehensum*] by this knowledge, not that it can be run through in succession [*pertransibile*]." For other texts on God's knowledge of an actually infinite multitude of possibles, see *De Veritate*, q. 2, art. 9; q. 20, art. 4, ad 1um; *Summa contra Gentes*, I, 69; *Quaestiones Quodlibetales*, q. 3, art. 2, ad 1um.
5. *Scriptum super Sententiis*, ed. Mandonnet, Lib. III, dist. 14, art. 2, q. 2, sol. 2: "For those things that are, or will be, or were at any time . . . although the essence through which He sees is one, since He sees them through distinct ideal 'reasons' or ideas [*ideales rationes*], therefore He has distinct knowledge about them. But those things which neither are, nor will be, nor ever were . . . and yet could have been present or past or future, since they do not exist in themselves, have no distinction in themselves, and do not exist save in the power of God, where they are one. Hence there cannot

be different respects according to which the intelligible content of
these possibles is distinguished. And therefore God does not know
them through distinct ideas, but through the knowledge of His
own power, in which they are."

6. A. D. Sertillanges, o.p., *Le Christianisme et les philosophes*
(Paris: Aubier, 1941), pp. 273–76. Sertillanges, one of the truly
great Thomistic metaphysicians, came out in these remarkable
pages to say publicly what it appears he was not allowed to say
earlier—namely, that much of St. Thomas' doctrine on divine ideas
is a concession to the Augustinian tradition, which he should not
have gone along with if faithful to his own principles, and in particular should never have held that God knew *distinctly all* the
pure possibles. The proper way to speak would be to say that there
is in God an infinity of *possibility,* not an infinity of *possibles.*

COMMENT ON
PROFESSOR SMITH'S PAPER

I find John Smith's paper not only insightful and stimulating, but also surprising for its closeness to my own thought development. First there is the common stimulus to our reflection in the identical article by Paul Tillich, "Two Philosophies of Religion." It was the inspiration for the whole first chapter of my *The Philosophical Approach to God*, where I developed an inner path of intellectual ascent to God through the dynamism of the spirit toward the Infinite, inspired by Transcendental Thomism's interpretation of St. Thomas.

I came to this article much later than John. Through the example of Plotinus—that remarkable synthesis of an inner spiritual ascent and an "outer" metaphysical argument—and the careful analysis of the Transcendental Thomists, plus Blondel, I had early come to see the possibility of an interior ascent of the mind to God through the inner dynamism of the spirit (both intellect for being as true and the will for being as good). But Tillich's article jolted me into the necessity of deploying both arguments as complementary in order to capture the full relationship of reality to its Source. In an age like St. Thomas', when objective metaphysical argument was highly esteemed, under the impulse of the new Aristotelian scientific approach, the cosmological type of argument might have been enough. In our own day, however, when the role of the subject has become so central, as the culmination of a long drift in Western thought since Descartes, and where we find it difficult to commit our minds to any intellectual structure without some existential personal involvement, the inner path is indispensable.

But so is the outer or more "objective" metaphysical path from the structure of all being. For by the inner path alone

I can indeed reach *my* God, the infinite Source of goodness and truth *for me*; but it is not clear that without some further broadening of my base I can discern God explicitly as the *ultimate Source of all being*, including my own. And without that, the God of the inner life and the God of the cosmos do not yet clearly coincide, which they must for our complete intellectual satisfaction. So I agree thoroughly with John on the need for the two paths and their harmonious complementarity.

I also agree with him on the possibility of bringing the two approaches closer together through the common notion of the *presence of God* revealed through both, though in different ways. It is on this notion of God revealed as present through the cosmological argument—what I myself would prefer to call the "metaphysical argument"—that I would like to focus the rest of my comments. Here, I think, John is onto something really important that has been missed or lost sight of by many modern critics of the approach from the cosmos as a whole. But he does not seem to me to be fully aware of the rich resources in the Thomistic metaphysics of causality for developing this point. At least he has not done so in this paper; so I would like to complete what he has begun so well.

The first point is his interpretation of the methodology of St. Thomas, in which he sees the dethroning of *sapientia* or wisdom (mediating the presence of God in the soul) for a purely finite, this-worldly inferential type of knowledge he calls *scientia*, which showed no signs of the divine presence. There is indeed something in this interpretation and implied criticism, especially as it applies to Aristotle. But there is another, more neglected, quite un-Aristotelian side of St. Thomas' epistemology. This is the notion of the "natural light" of the mind, with its inherent first principles waiting to be explicitly activated by sense experience, as a natural, built-in, permanent *finite participation in the Divine Light itself*. This is his reinterpretation, in the metaphysical mode of participation, of the Augustinian illumination theory, which he is always careful not simply to reject, but to reinterpret—not as a direct transitory intervention of the divine

activity in each of our acts of knowing, but rather as an abiding, built-in, *individual* personal participation in the Divine
Light or Intelligence itself.

Why did he gently lay aside the direct activity of God in the
created mind? Because of the dangerous implications he saw
already being drawn by medieval Augustinians who had con-
flated the Avicennan doctrine of one Agent Intellect for all
men with the Augustinian notion of divine illumination, and
also following from Augustine's *argument* for the need of divine illumination. For if all creatures, including spiritual
intelligences, are created and finite, then they are necessarily
mutable in their core, and in line with the ancient Platonic
tradition nothing mutable can truly know the immutable.
Hence no created mind by its own power can know, not only
God, but any immutable truth, such as those of mathematics,
as immutably true. Hence God must intervene with an *uncreated* act of knowing or help to knowing, in order to close
the gap. But if this is taken literally, St. Thomas argued, then
no act of knowing truth can really be our own personal act of
knowing, but only of God himself knowing in and through
us; nor can we be in control of our own acts of assisted knowing, since a higher Agent is involved whose will we cannot
control.

This was all too close to the doctrine of Avicenna that
there was only one divine Agent Intellect that thought in and
through all men. St. Thomas in rebuttal sounds the clarion call
for the restoration of knowing as *my* personal act, under the
control of *my will* as a genuine autonomous person: *"This*
individual man here [we would say today, "I"] knows when
he wills to."[1] The act of knowing of a responsible person must
be *his own* act and not God's; and this requires that each man
have a permanent, built-in natural power of his own to know
all the truths he can know, immutable or not. Otherwise he
would be a failed nature, with no intrinsic power to do his
own characteristic action as a human nature. But the natural
light of the mind is itself a direct and very lofty participation
in the power of the Divine Intelligence, the Light of the world

and of all minds as their Source. Herein lies the source of man's great dignity as an *image of God,* and not merely a vestige like the rest of nature. Since Aristotle firmly rejected all participation of the lower in the higher world, this is not the Aristotelian dimension of Thomas' epistemology, but the result of the fusion of Aristotelian nature with Neoplatonic participation theory, mediated here through Augustine. This finite imprint of the Divine Intelligence on the human can be made the basis for an inner dialectic of ascent to God as present to the soul (though a hidden presence) in the mode of an original to its image. But most expositions of Thomistic epistemology unfortunately leave out this participation or image dimension of St. Thomas' own full theory of knowledge.[2]

Now for the second and really more central point, the one I am especially interested in. This is the notion of "presence" of the higher cause in its effect, which John Smith rather tantalizingly suggests is latent in the notion of efficient causality and could be developed, but which he himself does not go on to work out in this paper. I would like to take up from where he left off. For John is onto something very important here. And I am not entirely sure he is aware of how much of what he is calling for is already contained quite explicitly in St. Thomas' authentic doctrine of efficient causality, almost entirely lost in Hume's reduction of causality to nothing more than the extrinsic relation of antecedent–consequent events in linear sequence. Let me explain.

John is quite right in saying that in order to find the presence of God latent in His created effects we must get beyond the model of cause and effect that has become dominant since Hume and Kant—namely, that of a regularly repeated pattern of two distinct observable events, antecedent and consequent, following each other in purely linear temporal sequence, with no further bond between them than this purely extrinsic one of juxtaposition in time. Since the relation is purely extrinsic, based on temporal sequence, there can be no question of any presence of the cause in the effect, nor of any similarity be-

COMMENTS

tween cause and effect because of their relation, since the cause is not conceived of as actually doing anything positive or giving anything of itself to its effect. The relation is one of spatial and temporal juxtaposition, not ontological sharing or self-communication.

But the Thomistic relation of cause and effect is a much older and deeper doctrine. The notion of cause stems originally from the Greek law courts, where it expressed the result of a judge's passing *judgment* based on the evidence—not on empirical observation by himself—as to who was the person guilty (αἴτιος) of a given crime. From meaning the guilty one, it broadened to mean whoever was *responsible* for something happening; from there it became generalized to mean *whatever was responsible* for the being or coming into being of something, either in whole or in part.[3] This generalized abstract notion of cause (αἰτία) became fixed in Aristotle, and for subsequent thought in the West roughly till Hume (with forerunners in late medieval Nominalism). In Aristotle it was still restricted to the cause of *becoming*, or change in being, either accidental or substantial. With the medieval Christian and Arabic thinkers, seeking to account for creation out of nothing, it was deepened to become the cause, not merely of the becoming, but of the *being itself* of the effect (from *causa fiendi* to *causa essendi*). The notion of efficient cause, therefore, in this long tradition broken by Hume, is really the objective correlate of the unrestricted drive of the inquiring mind to understand; it shifts analogously to express *whatever is needed* to fulfill the exigency of intelligibility, the *sufficient reason*, for the existence or coming into being of something, in whole or in part. God as ultimate Source of all being is the supreme instantiation of such a metaphysical sufficient reason.

In the light of this tradition of efficient cause interpreted analogously as cause of being in any way needed, the modern objection raised by John Smith, which he seems a bit ambiguously to feel sympathy with—namely, that a finite effect can lead us only to a finite cause so that we can never leap from a finite chain of causes into the Infinite—loses all force, and would indeed have astonished St. Thomas and other medieval philosophers. For it is precisely because one can show that *no* finite cause, as finite, can be the ultimate sufficient reason for the existence of any being that in the last analysis an efficient cause is needed that is *not* finite but Infinite; only such a cause can be ultimately *the responsible one* for being itself. Thus the inquiring mind at work, on the subjective side, and the adequate efficient cause, on the objective side, are but two sides of the same coin in such a metaphysical tradition.

Now more directly to the *presence* of the efficient cause in its effect. In this Aristotelian tradition, deepened by St. Thomas to the level of existence itself, one of the central—and I think most truly insightful—points in the analysis of the nature of efficient causality is the location of *action*, as a category of being. Since action is the actual bringing about of the new being in the effect by the efficient cause, it cannot be located ontologically back in the cause, since it is not the cause which is being changed but the effect; nor can it be floating somewhere in between. It must be therefore *in the effect* itself, as *from* the cause: *actio est in passo,* as the medievals translated it. The action of the efficient cause is the communication of being in some way to the effect within that effect; it is the dynamic presence of the cause in the effect, where cause and effect become one while the act of causality lasts, not in a unity of essence but in a dynamic continuum of force or energy; as I like to put it more poetically, it is the "ecstasy of the cause in the effect."[4]

It follows from this, St. Thomas tells us, that every cause must necessarily be present in its effect as long as the act of causality perdures. In created causes this presence is only momentary or transitory, since created finite causes can only be the cause of the becoming or change in a being, its *becoming such and such,* not its radical *act of being* itself. If we apply this doctrine to God, however, the situation radically changes. Since He is constantly sustaining the very act of existence of all creatures, He must be constantly present in all things in what is most intimate to each one. Hence, St. Thomas says, with just a touch of emotion, God is indeed present in all beings, and intimately indeed (*et intime*).[5] Here we have the secret of why St. Thomas' arguments to the existence of God from efficient causality, if pushed to their metaphysical depth at the level of existence itself, reveal to us, just as John Smith has suggested, the abiding inner presence of God in the entire cosmos, a presence as active giver and sustainer of their very being—i.e., their own active presence in the universe—a divine presence at first hidden on the observational level but unveiled by the metaphysical analysis of their need for an adequate efficient cause of their being at the deepest level. This deepening of the working of the efficient cause all the way to the level of existence, with the notion of the presence of the cause to the effect, is unfortunately not done by St. Thomas in his Five Ways, but only later, in the final metaphysical ascent to God as Infinite and One through participation.[6] This whole dimension of Thomas' thought is missed by those who take the all too heavily Aristotelian Five Ways as the adequate paradigm by itself of St. Thomas' cosmological approach to God.

Thus it ends up that for St. Thomas, at least (and for myself as firmly planted in this tradition), John Smith is right on the beam—*perhaps* more Thomistically than he suspected—in his central contention that the two paths to the existence of God, the inner and the outer, both turn out to be complementary paths to discover the presence of God to His creation, both to the soul within and to the cosmos without (or perhaps better, enveloping the within). As a Hindu Vedantist would say, the *Atman* is the *Brahman*.

NOTES

1. *De Spiritualibus Creaturis*, art. 10.

2. For this whole participation doctrine of the natural light of the mind, cf. *De Spiritualibus Creaturis*, art. 10; *Quaestiones de Anima*, art. 5; *Summa contra Gentes*, II, 76, n. 19; *Summa Theologiae*, I, q. 79, art. 5; q. 84, art. 5; *De Veritate*, q. 1, art. 4 ad 5um; q. 11, art. 1 ad 13um: "And therefore the fact that anything is

known with certitude is derived from the light of reason with which we are endowed from within by God and by which God speaks within us." See also the fine exposition of why St. Thomas felt he had to criticize the current Augustinian divine illumination theory: E. Gilson, "Sur quelques difficultés de l'illumination augustinienne," *Revue Néoscolastique*, 36 (1934), 321–31. St. Thomas' critique was so convincing that one by one all the thirteenth-century Augustinians abandoned the position, until the definitive coup de grâce was given by Duns Scotus, himself a Franciscan.

3. Cf. H. Boeder, "Origine et préhistoire de la question philosophique de l'AITION," *Revue des Sciences Philosophiques et Théologiques*, 40 (1956), 421–43, a fascinating article.

4. Cf. F. Meehan, *Efficient Causality in Aristotle and St. Thomas* (Washington: Catholic University of America Press, 1940); L. De Raeymaeker, *Philosophy of Being* (St. Louis: Herder, 1956), chap. on causality.

5. *Summa Theologiae*, I, q. 8, art. 1.

6. I have developed these truly metaphysical arguments from participation, which I consider to be the most authentic Thomas and far superior in depth and strength to the Five Ways, in Chap. II of my *The Philosophical Approach to God*. It is an interesting and puzzling question why he did not make use of this powerful participation metaphysics, his own unique synthesis of Aristotle and Neoplatonism, more explicitly in the Five Ways. It may well be that he wanted to make use of the more commonly known Aristotelian arguments of his time, or, as Gilson suggests, that he wished to begin all his arguments, in this work for "beginners," from evidence immediately available to the senses. His own metaphysics of participation is hardly that.

PUBLICATIONS OF
WILLIAM NORRIS CLARKE, S. J.

BOOK

The Philosophical Approach to God: A Contemporary Neo-Thomist Perspective. Winston-Salem: Wake Forest University, 1979.

ARTICLES

"The Role of Unity in the Philosophy of St. Augustine." *The Modern Schoolman,* 17 (1940), 70–74.

"The Notion of Human Liberty in Suarez." *The Modern Schoolman,* 19 (1942), 32–35.

"Industrial Democracy in Belgium." *Social Order,* 2:49–68; repr. *The American Catholic Sociological Review,* 10 (1949), 229–57.

"Recent European Trends in Metaphysics." *Proceedings of the Jesuit Philosophical Association,* 12 (1950), 48–73.

"The Limitation of Act by Potency: Aristotelianism or Neoplatonism?" *New Scholasticism,* 26 (1952), 167–94; repr. *Ciencia y Fe,* 8 (1952), 7–34.

"The Meaning of Participation in St. Thomas." *Proceedings of the American Catholic Philosophical Association,* 26 (1952), 147–57.

"Christian Humanism for Today." *Social Order,* 3 (1953), 269–88.

"The Platonic Heritage of Thomism." *The Review of Metaphysics,* 8 (1954), 105–24.

"Colloquium on the Idea of Creation." *The Review of Metaphysics,* 9 (1956), 475–77.

"What Is Really Real?" In *Progress in Philosophy,* ed. James A. McWilliams. Milwaukee: Bruce, 1955. Pp. 61–90.

Translation of "Being and Subjectivity" by Joseph de Finance, s.j. *Cross Currents,* 6 (1956), 163–78.

179

"On the Being of Creatures: A Critique of Gerald Phelan's Paper." *Proceedings of the American Catholic Philosophical Association,* 31 (1957), 128–32.

"St. Thomas and Platonism." *Thought,* 32 (1957), 437–43.

"End of the Modern World?" *America,* 99 (1958), 106–108. Repr. as a pamphlet by America Press.

"Christians Confront Technology." *America,* 101 (1959), 252–58.

"New Images of Man." *America,* 102 (1959), 232–36.

"Infinity in Plotinus." *Gregorianum,* 40 (1959), 75–98.

"The Possibles Revisited." *The New Scholasticism,* 34 (1960), 79–102.

"Linguistic Analysis and Natural Theology." *Proceedings of the American Catholic Philosophical Association,* 34 (1960), 110–26.

"Our Experience of God." *International Philosophical Quarterly,* 1 (1960), 168–73.

"Causality and Time." In *Experience, Existence and the Good: Essays in Honor of Paul Weiss,* ed. Irwin C. Lieb. Carbondale: Southern Illinois University Press, 1961. Pp. 143–57.

"On Professors Ziff, Niebuhr, and Tillich." In *Religious Experience and Truth: A Symposium,* ed. Sidney Hook. New York: New York University Press, 1961. Pp. 224–30.

"System: A New Category of Being." *Proceedings of the Jesuit Philosophical Association,* 24 (1962), 143–57.

"Is the West God's Civilization?" *America,* 106 (1962), 853–56.

"Cultural Dimensions of the New Leisure." In *The Ethical Aftermath of Automation,* ed. Francis Quinn, s.j. Westminster, Md.: Newman Press, 1962. Pp. 199–212.

"Authority and Private Judgment." In *In the Eyes of Others,* ed. Robert Gleason, s.j. New York: Macmillan, 1962. Pp. 61–85.

"Technology and Man: A Christian Vision." *Technology and Culture,* 3 (1962), 422–42.

"Current Views on the Intrinsic Nature of Philosophy." In *Christian Wisdom and Christian Formation,* ed. Barry McGannon, s.j. New York: Sheed & Ward, 1964. Pp. 141–63.

"Is Understanding Religion Compatible with Believing It?" In *Faith and the Philosophers*, ed. John Hick. New York: St. Martin's Press, 1964. Pp. 134–46.

"The Self in Eastern and Western Thought: The Wooster Conference." *International Philosophical Quarterly*, 6 (1966), 101–109.

"American Philosophy and Language about God." In *Christian Philosophy and Religious Renewal*, ed. George McLean, O.M.I. Washington: Catholic University of America Press, 1966. Pp. 39–73.

"The Future of Thomism." In *New Themes in Christian Philosophy*, ed. Ralph McInerny. Notre Dame: University of Notre Dame Press, 1968. Pp. 187–207.

"The Self as Source of Meaning in Metaphysics." *The Review of Metaphysics*, 21 (1967), 587–614.

"Reflections on the Fourteenth International Congress of Philosophy." *International Philosophical Quarterly*, 9 (1969), 134–41.

"How the Philosopher Can Give Meaning to Language about God." In *The Idea of God: Philosophical Perspectives*, edd. Edward H. Madden, Rollo Handy, Marvin Farber. Springfield, Ill.: Thomas, 1969. Pp. 1–27, 37–42.

"On Facing Up to the Truth about Human Truth." *Proceedings of the American Catholic Philosophical Association*, 43 (1969), 1–13.

"The Nature of Conscience in Philosophical Perspective." In *Conscience: Its Freedom and Limitations*, ed. William C. Bier, s.j. New York: Fordham University Press, 1971. Pp. 357–68.

"A Curious Blindspot in the Anglo-American Tradition of Anti-Theistic Argument." *The Monist*, 54 (1970), 181–200.

"A New Look at the Immutability of God." In *God Knowable and Unknowable*, ed. Robert J. Roth, s.j. New York: Fordham University Press, 1973. Pp. 43–72.

"What Cannot Be Said in St. Thomas' Essence–Existence Doctrine." *The New Scholasticism*, 48 (1974), 19–39.

"What is Most and Least Relevant in St. Thomas' Metaphysics Today?" *International Philosophical Quarterly*, 14 (1974), 411–34.

"Interpersonal Dialogue as Key to Realism." In *Person and Community*, ed. Robert J. Roth, s.j. New York: Fordham University Press, 1975. Pp. 141–54.

"Analogy and the Meaningfulness of Language about God: A Reply to Kai Nielson." *The Thomist*, 40 (1976), 61–95.

"Freedom as Value." In *Freedom and Value*, ed. Robert O. Johann. New York: Fordham University Press, 1976. Pp. 1–19.

"Spiritual Experience and Metaphysical Interpretation." In *Man and Nature*, ed. George McLean, o.m.i. Calcutta: Oxford University Press, 1978. Pp. 188–97.

"Death and the Meaning of Life in the Christian Tradition." *Sixth International Conference on Unity of Science*. New York: International Cultural Foundation, 1977. Pp. 493–504.

"The Role of Essence in St. Thomas' Essence–Existence Doctrine: Positive or Negative Principle? A Dispute within Thomism." *Atti del Congresso Internazionale di San Tommaso*. Naples: Edizioni Domenicane, 1981. Pp. 9–15.

"The Philosophical Importance of Doing One's Autobiography." *Proceedings of the American Catholic Philosophical Association*, 54 (1980), 17–25.

"The Natural Roots of Religious Experience." *Religious Studies*, 17 (1981), 511–23.

"The Problem of the Reality and Multiplicity of the Divine Ideas in Christian Neoplatonism." In *Neoplatonism and Christian Thought*, ed. Dominic J. O'Meara. Albany: State University of New York Press, 1982. Pp. 109–27.

"Action as the Self-Revelation of Being: A Central Theme in the Thought of St. Thomas." In *History of Philosophy in the Making*, ed. Linus Thro, s.j. Washington: University Press of America, 1982. Pp. 63–80.

"The Metaphysics of Religious Art." In *Graceful Reason: Essays in Honor of Joseph Owens, C.Ss.R.*, ed. Lloyd P. Gerson. Toronto: Pontifical Institute of Mediaeval Studies, 1983. Pp. 303–14.

"To Be Is to be Self-Communicative: St. Thomas' Vision of Personal Being." *Theology Digest*, 33 (1986), 441–54.

"Form and Matter" and "Substance and Accident." In *The New Dictionary of Theology*, edd. Joseph A. Komonchak, Mary Collins, Dermot A. Lane. Wilmington: Glazier, 1987. Pp. 398–404 and 986–90.